1000 FOR 2000

Predictions for the New Millennium

John Hogue

HarperSanFrancisco
A Division of HarperCollinsPublishers

1000 FOR 2000: *Predictions for the New Millennium.* Copyright © 1999 by John
Hogue. All rights reserved. Printed in the United States of America. No part of
this book may be used or reproduced in any manner whatsoever without
written permission except in the case of brief quotations embodied in critical
articles and reviews. For information address HarperCollins Publishers, 10 East
53rd Street, New York, NY 10022.

HarperCollins books may be purchased for educational, business, or sales
promotional use. For information please write: Special Markets Department,
HarperCollins Publishers, Inc., 10 East 53rd Street, New York, NY 10022.
HarperCollins Web Site: http://www.harpercollins.com

HarperCollins®, ⬛®, and HarperSanFrancisco™ are
trademarks of HarperCollins Publishers Inc.

FIRST EDITION
Designed by Joseph Rutt

Library of Congress Cataloging-in-Publication Data
Hogue, John
1000 for 2000 : predictions for the new millennium / John Hogue.—1st ed.
p.   cm.
ISBN 0-06-251806-2 (pbk.)
1. Twenty-first century—forecasts.   2. Prophecies (Occultism)
I. Title.   II. Title: One thousand for two thousand.
BF1809.H63   1999
133.3—DC21   99-28517

99 00 01 02 03 ❖/RRD 10 9 8 7 6 5 4 3 2 1

To Vipassana, my mother, who received far
more than a thousand kicks from me before
the moment she laughed and I was born.
And to the Blessed One gestating in both of us
since then.

CONTENTS

INTRODUCTION:
NEW YEAR'S 2000:
DOOMSDAY,
BLOOMSDAY,
OR
BUFFOON'S DAY?

ONE THOUSAND YEARS AGO, millennium fever was an isolated phenomenon seen only in Europe. Visions of the world coming to an end in flames didn't disturb the civilizations of South and East Asia. When India entered the last month of the old millennium, the only trace of wide-ranging fires came from farmers burning off leaf refuse from the summer monsoon season. The Islamic year overlapping the Christian calendar years of 999–1000 was a doomsday dud. Judgment Day came and went without much fanfare sometime around the year 390 after the Hegira. On the other hand, Muslims living in Palestine at that time did record a marked increase in tourism profits from a larger than normal influx of Christian pilgrims coming to Jerusalem to pray and pay their final respects to the Holy Land.

The year launching the second Christian millennium wasn't even a blip in the 400,000-year Kali Yuga (epoch) of the Hindu calendar, and Polynesians sailing the South Pacific in great catamaran canoes were clueless that the world was coming to an end.

They discovered New Zealand, and thus the year that should have ended the world completed the final stage of the greatest migration and nautical exodus in history. A thousand-plus native American nations took no note of anything doom-laden for that year. They didn't expect the harbinger of their apocalypse to appear anytime soon. Indeed the foretold "lost white brother," carrying the ill omen of the cross over the Eastern ocean, didn't sail over the Atlantic for another half a millennium. Some daring Vikings did sail westward in the year 1000, but they found neither the edge nor the end of the world. They discovered the New World instead and for a time established colonies in Labrador and Newfoundland.

The only place where millennium fever burned brightly at the approach of the year 1000 was in the Christian kingdoms of medieval Europe. Many believed apocryphal stories that said the first day of the thousandth year after the birth of Christ was the day the world would end. Throughout the year 999 a medieval version of a Y2K panic seized the bankers and record keepers facing Y1K. If number "00" in a computer can erase someone's bank account in our near future, then a year ending in "000" saw people a thousand years ago wiping out their bank accounts in extreme acts of charity. The indebted believed they gained brownie points in heaven by rubbing out the records of moneys owed to them by debtors. Many burghers went as far as throwing away their ledger books and closing their businesses. Some of the rich gave their wealth away so they could face God in a blessed and dirt-poor state. Farmers abandoned their crops. "What need will there be of food next year when there will be no *next year?*" they reasoned. Toward the end of the year commerce and agriculture in Europe generally shut down, with the result that many regions suffered doomsday-style bouts of famine and social chaos. The classes mingled in great pilgrimages to Rome and other holy places in Europe, and ultimately one saw mixed multitudes of nobles, merchants, and peasants surging all the way to Jerusalem.

By autumn of 999, millions of the backsliding faithful raised the gain of their prayers and intensified their acts of Christian virtue—some to the point of whipping themselves into a frenzy of penance. One saw armies of flagellants roaming the frosty countryside of Europe toward the end of December. One could follow their trails of blood through fields and fetid medieval city streets. Mobs cornered and killed the misfits and purported witches, they hanged tax collectors and a few unlucky rich merchants, and of course they burned a lot of Jews in a rush to gain one last bit of good merit before the angel Gabriel blew his horn.

In the final hour of New Year's Eve, Pope Sylvester II led thousands of cowering and kneeling believers in a Mass in Rome's pre-Vatican and ancient St. Peter's Basilica. Eyewitnesses report that as midnight struck the revelers of revelation didn't exactly mark the new millennium with party horns and bawdy, inebriated shouts of "Happy New Year!" The crowd screamed in terror and several people in the basilica dropped dead from fright. Yet January 1, 1000, came and went like any other day, and this astounded everyone in Europe from the pope to the lowest peasant. Why hadn't the world ended? Theologians eventually reasoned that God must have postponed the end of the world until the year 2000.

The first day of the new one-thousand-year reprieve from doom found many stunned burghers rummaging through refuse heaps to find their discarded ledgers. The new millennium's gray dawn light illuminated the way for farmers wandering over the countryside searching for the livestock they released a few weeks earlier. On New Year's Day, people came down to earth again, the class system was back in force, and local merchants were a tad less charitable. They no longer gave their goods away and debts rose out of their graves demanding payment.

History has its constants. A thousand years ago, people couldn't count their millenniums any better than they can today. The average embarrassed and bewildered adventists of the Middle Ages were probably too busy burying those who either died from fright or had succumbed to infections festering in the wounds of the flagellant's lash to get a basic lesson in math. Perhaps a day of chasing the liberated pigs and geese on an empty stomach, made so by crops and meat stocks left to rot, made the people too irritable at the close of New Year's Day 1000 to understand that there were still 364 more days to muddle through before the real end of the millennium took place and Quasimodo rang in January 1, 1001. A thousand years later people are just as hypnotized by the three zeros, thinking they stand for the ultimate rather than the penultimate year of a new epoch, and they schedule their parties one year too soon.

Being bad at math has its advantages. I, for one, plan to party on December 31, 1999, and party again on December 31, 2000.

Party as we might, this time around the potential for an epidemic of millennium fever will be global, thanks to easy access to information and the adoption by the whole world of the Judeo-Christian calendar. The deadline date of December 31, 1999, already compels most people around the world to stockpile either champagne for the greatest party in history or bottled water, freeze-dried food, and ammo in their survivalist bunker to meet the dreaded Y2K—the end of the world.

A thousand years of advances in technology not only make our present world that proverbially smaller global village, but easy access to information—whether one is searching the Web for the best vacation plan or bomb plan—could also make everyone in the year 2000 a bigger target for doomsday-mongers.

Fundamentalist fanatics have had another thousand years to feast and fatten their psychoses on apocryphal interpretations—not only from Christian eschatology, mind you, but from every other religion's doom-laden predictions—and this time they can preach to a global audience. In the past, medieval doomsayers saw signs in the heavens that the end was near; today, televangelists project their own versions of current events through mass-hypnosis on their TV audiences. Where millennium fanatics of the Dark Ages did little more than regional harm to others, their descendants at the threshold of the year 2000 form cults that spray Sarin gas in Tokyo subways, immolate their communities in Waco, Texas, or plan terrorist attacks in Jerusalem in the hope that righteous violence will bring on the end of the world and the appearance of the messiah.

All eschatological arguments aside, this time around—or better, this "potential" end time around—we stand at the close of another millennium's worth of abuse and buildup of social tensions that could explode, at least coincidentally, either at or a few decades beyond the year 2000. After a thousand more New Year's celebrations, there is less wilderness to trash and less arable acreage to feed our exploding numbers. A thousand years ago, people in western Europe may have had nightmares of the world ending, but the few hundred million people living at the last millennium never knew our clear and present nightmare of six billion people consuming with abandon a world of finite resources, finite food and water reserves; nor could prophecy interpreters of that era dream there would be a day when the civilization might simply collapse from its own excesses, rather than from the swipe of God's hand. A thousand years ago the animals didn't disappear from the earth as foreseen, but a thousand years later animal species *are* disappearing in the greatest mass extinction since the dino doomsday some 65,000 millennia before.

Medieval peasants waited in vain for angels to drop their seven vials of God's pestilential wrath. Little did they know that biblical plague prophecies such as those from Revelation 16 have far more objective parallels at the onset of our new millennium. Today the vials of pestilence appear as new viruses, such as the blood plagues of AIDS, Ebola, and Hepatitis A, B, and C. New antibiotic-resistant germs exist today that echo the words of Zechariah 14:12 and eat flesh right off the bone. The medieval world was filthy, but there was no steady buildup of global toxic pollution or radioactive fallout from nuclear disasters. Its people didn't face unprecedented health problems from the long-term effects of a half century of over sixteen hundred atmospheric and underground atomic bomb tests poisoning the world as we rehearsed Armageddon.

The medieval end-time penitents stared into the harmless blue screens of benign and pollution-free skies to compute their illusory and foreboding projections of angelic and demonic armies hurling shooting stars at each other. A thousand years later our polluted modern skies do threaten us with global warming. It seems the heavens are heating up and disrupting our weather just as the prophet Isaiah said they would, and we could be a few decades away from warmer seas melting our ice caps and flooding our coastlines. Perhaps the skies of the year 2000 won't see any demons or angels spear-chucking comets; however, the skies will have wounds and they are growing larger each year. The gashes called ozone holes are yawning wider, and it is certain that the new millennium sun will rise every day in the coming fifty years to bombard us with ever more dangerous arrows of invisible cosmic radiation that could disrupt our crops and bring cataracts to our eyes and cancer to our skin.

The Y1K era's spin on prophecies of doom better resembles the foreboding trends of our modern times, but so do alternative prophecies of "bloomsday." Perhaps the many accomplishments of modern times fulfill the visions composed over a thousand years ago of a new heaven and earth rising from the destruction of the old models. Imagine the Dark Age diviner coming across images of our clean cities or our fantastic flying machines, cars, and ocean-going vessels. Picture the awe and amazement the short-lived and chronically diseased medieval peasants would experience as they gazed for the first time at our louse-free clothes, our healthy and clean bodies; see them salivating at the luscious colors and bounty of our maggot-free foods; imagine how they would gasp in wonder at the miracle of our glass-sheathed and sparkling cities that tower higher than New Jerusalem. They might believe we are the transubstantiated souls dwelling in kingdom come after God's will is done at the Final Day of Judgment.

In the year 2000 we will discover fantastic things the people of the last millennium could never have fathomed. The Hubble telescope shows us new heavens and new earths. Human eyes in space look down upon our planet as it was never seen before, and our understanding of how fragile our home in the universe is deepens. We see how interconnected are its people, and perhaps that revelation is greater and holds more promise than any dire warning in the Book of Revelation. If we are millennium revelers standing on the brink of global disasters as foretold, so too are we more capable of performing miracles that can forestall the end of the world.

I've been collecting predictions from every one of those biblically defined four corners of this round world for nearly thirty years. I have found that for every doom-laden potential future set to begin at or shortly after the year 2000, there is an opposite *bloom*-laden alternative. Prophecies foreseeing the flowering of a new millennium of peace and tranquillity exist. The future is fluid and not preordained. The appearances in every prophetic tradition of either-or visions are too numerous to ignore. Prophecy is unborn history enclosed in a womb of potential. The present day is ever like the suffering yet hopeful mother gestating the future's birth by her present decisions and actions, whether positive or negative in nature and intent. Metaphorically speaking, we all mother the future by what we do today. If the future is the outcome of our actions, then prophecies sometimes can give us a nudge like a baby's kick. If we but listen, we will know how to give birth to the right future.

1000 for 2000 presents to you one thousand kicks from the baby called the new millennium.

This book is unlike any of the last seven I've written on the subject of millennial prophecy. I have distilled my own interpretations down to a minimum, so that these quotes provide a cross section of a great discussion about the year 2000 and beyond. Gathered in the following pages we see the recorded visions of prophets from every era and every region in known history. They come together with as little of my commentary as possible, bringing forth testimonies of terror and of hope. Quotes assembled from every historical period and nearly every culture and corner of the world light upon these pages to make it appear as if the seers are sometimes building consensus for—and at other times are locked in a heated debate over—the collective destiny of the next thousand years.

No study of prophecy is without bias. Every interpreter leaves his or her intellectual and religious signature on the prophecies examined. I certainly admit to a temptation to include quotes that undermine or contradict the prophecies of any religious tradition that thinks its vision is the only true vision of tomorrow. In fairness to those prophets and their interpreters who might take offense at how I place their quotes, I have inserted a number of my own experimental prophecies into the mix for scrutiny. I willingly stick my divining-wand out there so that posterity's critics can have a go at me. The past accuracy of many of my published interpretations—along with the personally revealing and sometimes entertaining stories of my prophetic goofs—compel me to leave a record of predictions that will, at the worst, live long after me as an example of how ego, of both prophets and their interpreters, can color predictions and the fact that we shouldn't take their interpretations so seriously.

I believe a prophet who is always right is the greatest failure, because no one heeds the warning. I'm all for proving Nostradamus, the biblical prophets, Edgar Cayce, Mother Shipton, and the few hundred other seers in this book wrong by listening to their warnings and changing my life-negative contributions to the end of the world, if indeed there is an end.

I sincerely hope that today, and every day we live beyond January 1, 2000, will see us "enlightening up" and working together to make the dire prophecies in this book the stuff—and laughingstock—of fiction. Let each of us contribute enough love and awareness to make doomsday prophets truly great and exceedingly wrong.

A NOTE ON THE PROPHETS' QUOTES AND BYLINES

Prophecies that are direct quotes are followed by the author's name and the estimated date of the prophecy. I have provided the book title or verse number of the prophecy wherever possible.

If clarification of words in the translated prophecy is required, comments, additions, or changes are added in brackets ("[]"). Clarifications of grammar are also included. For example:

1. He [man] will come to take himself to the corner of Luna [the Moon] where he will be taken and placed on alien land.

NOSTRADAMUS (1557)

Les Propheties, *C9 Q65*

Any commentary follows directly after the byline in smaller note-like type.

AN OVERVIEW FOR THE NEW MILLENNIUM

OPENING PROPHECIES: DOOMSDAY *AND* BLOOMSDAY FORESEEN

1. Fortunate is the man who knows how to read the signs of the times, for that man shall escape many misfortunes, or at least be prepared to understand the blow.

> HERMES TRISMEGISTUS (a.d. 150–270)
> Asclepius III

2. We are living now in an age of ill-will, error, and decay. Whoever survives, without losing his moral qualities, has stood his fiery ordeal.

Seeress Regina, the German
Cassandra (early twentieth
century)

3. We believe that the present hour is a dread phase of the events foretold by Christ. It seems that darkness is about to fall on the world. Humanity is in the grip of a supreme crisis.

Pope Pius XII (1940)

4. The sword of death is approaching us now in the shape of plague and war more horrid than has been seen in the life of three generations.

Nostradamus (1555)
Preface to Les Propheties

We might infer here that the prophet is forecasting a conflict more horrendous than any suffered in the last ninety years, which would cover the previous two world wars!

5. [When] the great cycle of the centuries is renewed [2000]: It will rain blood, milk [the reddish-white, milky droplets of chemical weapons], famine, war and disease. In the sky will be seen a fire, dragging a trail of sparks [a missile].

Nostradamus (1555) *C2 Q46*

6. Plague, famine, death from military hands. The century and the age approaches it renewal [in 2000].

NOSTRADAMUS (1555) *C1 Q16*

7. It will appear at the time of the games of slaughter [computer-game violence?]—not far from the age of the great millennium [2000]—when the dead will come out of their graves [resurrection or enlightenment].

NOSTRADAMUS (1557) *C10 Q74*

8. This is what the Cabala says about the number 21, that is the twenty-first century: The World Accession to leadership, Temporal and Spiritual. Prosperity Cycle in Mundane Affairs.

Advancement of Backward People. Adept. Proper use of talent in arts, science, commerce. The power of Peace. The Hebrew Letter Schin, Planetary Ruler. The Luminous One, the Sun.

Tell me, readers, does this sound like Doomsday to you? To me, it sounds like the best, brightest, greatest century we will ever have: in other words, shades of paradise on Earth!

BEJAN DARUWALLA (1989), MODERN
INDIAN ASTROLOGER

9. Do not call me a prophet until the things I have foretold have come to pass.

ST. DON BOSCO (1841)

FOUR HORSEMEN OF THE APOCALYPSE

These are perhaps the four most famous allegories for doomsday.

The Traditional Version of the Four Horsemen for the Old Millennium

10. And I saw when the Lamb opened one of the [seven] seals, and I heard, as it were the noise of thunder, one of the four beasts saying, Come and see. And I saw, and behold a white horse: and he that sat on him had a bow; and a crown was given unto him: and he went forth conquering, and to conquer.

11. And when he had opened the second seal, I heard the second beast say, Come and see. And there went out another horse that was red: and power was given to him that sat thereon to take peace from the earth, and that they should kill one another: and there was given unto him a great sword.

12. And when he had opened the third seal, I heard the third beast say, Come and see. And I beheld, and lo a black horse; and he that sat on him had a pair of balances in his hand. And I heard a voice in the midst of the four beasts say, A measure of wheat for a penny, and three measures of barley for a penny; and see thou hurt not the oil and the wine.

13. And when he had opened the fourth seal, I heard the voice of the fourth beast say, Come and see. And I looked, and behold a pale horse: and his name that sat on him was Death, and Hell followed with him. And power was given unto them over the fourth part of the earth, to kill with sword, and with hunger, and with death, and with the beasts of the earth.

ST. JOHN OF PATMOS (a.d. 81–96)

Rev. 6:1–8

An Updated Version of the Horsemen and Horsewomen for the New Millennium

A new millennium may need a revised allegory of the Four Horsemen to make it topical for our changing times. For instance, it may be time to give equal opportunity to women and allow some of the Horsemen to be Horsewomen.

14. The First Hellrider of doomsday is a pregnant and starving woman armed with an empty begging bowl. She is called Overpopulation. She is the human breeding urge run amok and propagating a tomorrow of ecological holocaust. Through her, doomsday could be brought about by famine.

15. The Second Hellrider is a ravaged wiccan priestess, an archetype of Mother Nature, who is about to ride down her unseen attackers—namely, you, me, and six billion other eager breeders—with volcanic fire and lightning bolts. She is Earth Trauma, the harbinger of doomsday through an ecological breakdown of the Earth's climate and food chains.

16. The Third Hellrider is a knight with rodent features brandishing a giant syringe as a lance. He is called Lemming Syndrome, the harbinger of plagues. He is the stress of modern living, breaking down people's immune system and their will to live.

17. The Fourth Hellrider is the archetypal terrorist. He is hooded, and the green, glowing symbol for atomic energy hovers over his head like a halo. He wears a gas mask to protect himself from his own stolen biological and chemical weapons. He shoulders a tactical nuclear missile bought on the black market after the collapse of the Soviet Union. He carries a sinister radar dish as a shield and proudly displays a happy-face button on his chest. The button celebrates humanity's disarming dreams and illusion of safety from nuclear attack because the Cold War is over. The final Hellrider is called Third World's War—a future nuclear holocaust that may be more possible now because the Cold War has ended.

JOHN HOGUE (1994)
The Millennium Book of Prophecy

ECOLOGICAL DISASTER

OVERPOPULATION

In 1999 the population reached six billion. By the 2020s it will reach eight billion. By 2030 China will need, just to feed itself, an amount equal to all the grain produced in the world in 1999. Rapid population growth is the chief source of food insecurity, global ecological disaster, and social instability in the twenty-first century. The current lack of commitment by today's political leaders to pool together their forces and fight overpopulation could still bring on an all-out world war in the first decades of the twenty-first century. Unless we seek global solutions for global problems, the too numerous human race will fight World War III over dwindling food and water supplies.

18. Even now the world-cities of the Western Civilization are far from having reached the peak of their development. I see, long after A.D. 2000, cities laid out for ten to twenty million inhabitants, spread over enormous areas of countryside, with buildings that will dwarf the biggest of today's, and notions of traffic and communication that we should regard as fantastic to the point of madness.

OSWALD SPENGLER (1926)
The Decline of the West

19. In the 2020s a future pope commands all good Christians to abhor as an act of faith any means of contraception. As a result, the majority of the world suffering from the crushing catastrophe of overpopulation will condemn his ministry and his supporters. Demonstrations against the Catholic church would be seen the world over. The Vatican will be boycotted for promoting overpopulation.

JOHN HOGUE (1997) The Last Pope

20. By the year 2000, 50 percent of the population has to die simply of hunger. And just think, if 50 percent of the people die, what will be the situation of the living ones? There will be nobody even to carry their corpses to the graveyard; they will be rotting in your streets, in your neighborhoods, even in your own house. The whole world will have become a vast graveyard stinking of death.

OSHO (1987) The Razor's Edge

If current trends in population increase remain unchanged, Osho's vision could aptly describe the collapse of food and water sustainability in 2020–2050, rather than at 2000, when the planet will be burdened with an estimated eight to twelve billion people.

21. A further postponement of a global system of planned parenting could lead to the nightmare twenty or thirty years from now of armies occupying entire regions and gathering all child-bearing adults to be marched off into concentration camps for mass sterilizations.

JOHN HOGUE (1994)

22. Soil will be stimulated into maximum productivity, and the entire range of plants formerly considered weeds will be utilized for food or for clothing. These breakthroughs will enable the Earth to support comfortably fifty billion people.

DAVID GOODMAN CROLY (1888)
Glimpses of the Future

GLOBAL FAMINE

23. [At a time when there is a] great nation across the ocean that will be inhabited by peoples of different tribes and descent [America] . . . many nations will be scourged by want and famine.

HILDEGARD VON BINGEN (C. 1141)

24. For the hardships for this country have not begun yet, so far as the supply and demand for foods are concerned.

EDGAR CAYCE, PSYCHIC READING (1943)
No. 257–254

25. The great famine which I sense approaching will often turn [up] in various areas, then become worldwide.

NOSTRADAMUS (1555) C1 Q67

26. All public cult will be interrupted. A terrible and cruel famine will commence in the whole world and principally in the western regions, such as has never occurred since the world's beginning.

> João de Vatiguerro
> (thirteenth century)

27. How dreadful it will be in those days for pregnant women and nursing mothers.

> Jesus Christ (a.d. 30–33)
> *Matt. 24:19*

28. Great afflictions will come. . . . Nations will end in flames, and famine will annihilate millions.

> Francesca de Billante of Savoy
> (early twentieth century)

29. A great famine through a pestilent wave will extend its rain over the length of the Arctic pole.

> Nostradamus (1555) *C6 Q5*

30. Famine will spread over the nations.

> Brigham Young (d. 1877),
> Mormon prophet

31. Famine! . . . The century and the age approaches its renewal [the year 2000].

> Nostradamus (1555) *C1 Q16*

32. Famine [spreads] over the whole world. . . . Why, O Lord, dost Thou not stop all this with Thy arm?

> Prophecy of Premol (fifth century)

33. Long before the oceans permanently reclaim the planet's most arable river deltas, typhoons and tidal surges could leave most low-lying islands and vast tracts of coastal farmland sterilized with salt just a few years from now.

34. Rice comprises 90 percent of Asia's staple diet, and most of it is grown at sea level. A string of greenhouse typhoons and saltwater floods might wipe out some of Asia's rice belts, creating famine for billions.

JOHN HOGUE (1989)
The Millennium Book of Prophecy

35. [The great global famine] will be so vast and long lasting that [people] will grab roots from the trees and children from the breast.

NOSTRADAMUS (1555) *C1 Q67*

36. Whoever flees, should not look back. Whoever has two loafs of bread, will come through.

STORMBERGER (EIGHTEENTH CENTURY)

GLOBAL WARMING: THE ATMOSPHERE HEATS UP

The years 1990, 1995, 1997, and 1998 each set new all-time worldwide heat records. There is every indication so far that the year 1999 will top them all. The heat of global warming is already on. The worldwide emissions of fossil fuels such as carbon dioxide (CO_2) could mean a temperature rise of from 1.5 to 4.5 centigrade (2.7 to 8.1 degrees Fahrenheit) from the 1990s to the middle of the next century.

37. Changes of climate and all conditions relating to our planet are the direct outcome of the celestial influences brought to bear on it—the most important of all being the effect of "the Precession of the Equinoxes."

The "Precession of the Equinoxes" causes an alteration in the polar axis of the earth, and that in consequence the Sun retrogrades through every sign of the Zodiac, and in a period of time calculated as 2150 years passes out of one sign and enters another.

CHEIRO (1931)

Cheiro's World Predictions

Predictive astrology claims we are currently passing through the end of the Piscean Age and about to enter the 2150 years of the Age of Aquarius.

38. We have to expect a day when the balance of nature will be lost.

QUETZALCOATL (a.d. 947),

AZTEC MESSIAH

39. For, behold, the day cometh, that shall burn as an oven; and all the proud, yea, and all that do wickedly, shall be stubble: and the day that cometh shall burn them up.

MALACHI (c. 500–450 b.c.)

Mal. 4:1

40. The time has come . . . for destroying those who destroy the Earth.

ST. JOHN OF PATMOS (a.d. 81–96)

Rev. 11:18

41. All Western scientists, Western politicians, Western churches are preparing a big graveyard for the whole humanity.

> OSHO (1986)
> Socrates Poisoned Again

42. They will no longer love this world around us, this incomparable work of God, this glorious structure which he has built, this sum of good made up of things of many diverse forms, this instrument whereby the will of God operates in that which he has made, ungrudgingly favoring man's welfare, this combination and accumulation of all the manifold things that can call forth the veneration, praise, and love of the beholder.

> HERMES TRISMEGISTUS (a.d. 150–270)
> Asclepius III

43. [In the Kali Yuga] Earth will be venerated only for its mineral treasures.

> Vishnu Purana (c. A.D. 900), 24:26–27

The Kali Yuga is Hindu prophecy's name for the current, history-ending, dark age.

44. More and more people are starting to discover that what you have created together is very fragile. And all that you are continuously producing and consuming is eating away the planet and beings on its surface. The rich countries are devouring the most to uphold their material standard. And the poor countries have the rich as their idols. This creates an evil circle.

> AMBRES (1986),
> CHANNELED BY STURÉ JOHANSSON

45. The Earth dries up and withers, the world languishes and withers, the exalted of the Earth languish. The Earth is defiled by its people; they have disobeyed the laws, violated the statutes, and broken the everlasting covenant. Therefore a curse consumes the Earth; its people must bear their guilt. Therefore Earth's inhabitants are burned up, and very few are left.

ISAIAH (738–687 b.c.) *Isa. 24:4–6*

46. In truth, mankind today, with very few exceptions, is suffering from nature's punishment.

TAMO-SAN (1957), JAPANESE SEERESS
Moor the Boat

47. All nature will tremble because of the disorder and the misdeeds of men, which will rise to the very heavens.

PROPHECY OF LA SALETTE (1846),
ATTRIBUTED TO THE VIRGIN MARY

48. The more man despises nature the greater harm nature inflicts on him. The more speedily man tries to subjugate nature, the more speedily nature takes its revenge.

TAMO-SAN (1957) Moor the Boat

49. During the period of the hollow peace [the post–Cold War era], the seasons will change their natural character.

PROPHECY OF LA SALETTE (1846)

50. With these swords [rockets] it will be possible to cut up the skies [the ozone layer].

PASTOR BARTHOLOMAEUS
HOLZHAUSER (C. 1642)

51. And the fourth angel poured out his vial upon the sun; and power was given unto him to scorch men with fire. And men were scorched with great heat, and blasphemed the name of God.

ST. JOHN OF PATMOS (a.d. 81–96)
Rev. 16:8–9

52. The tropical rain forests support the sky—cut down the trees and disaster will follow.

SOUTH AMERICAN TRIBAL LEGEND

53. Fire will leap forth on the forests and meadows, wrapping all things there is a winding sheet of flame.

QUETZALCOATL (a.d. 947)

54. Then the earth no longer stands unshaken . . . all voices of the gods will of necessity be silenced and dumb: the fruits of the earth will rot: the soil will turn barren, and the very air will rot: the soil will turn barren, and the very air will sicken in sullen stagnation. After this manner will old age come upon the world.

HERMES TRISMEGISTUS (a.d. 150–270)
Asclepius III

55. As pollution continues, pure water will become more valuable than oil, and will be scarcer by far.

SPIRIT GUIDES OF RUTH MONTGOMERY
(1976) The World Before

56. Then shall the elements of all the world be desolate; air, earth, sea, flaming fire, and the sky and night, all days merge into one fire, and to one barren, shapeless mass to come.

Sibylline Oracles *(second century B.C.)*

GLOBAL WARMING: HOTHOUSE HURRICANES

Climatologists are concerned that warmer oceans in the twenty-first century will pump up the power of hurricanes by as much as 50 percent in the next twenty-five years. Hurricane Mitch careened into Central America during the hurricane season of 1998, killing up to 20,000 people and flattening the infrastructure of Nicaragua, Belize, and Honduras. Is this a precursor of things to come?

57. A powerful wind will rise in the north carrying heavy fog and the densest of dust by God's command, and it will fill their throats and eyes so that they will put an end to their savagery and be stricken with a great fear.

HILDEGARD VON BINGEN (C. 1141)

58. The great city of the maritime ocean, surrounded by a swamp of crystal: In the winter solstice and the spring will be tried by a terrible wind.

NOSTRADAMUS (1557) C9 Q48

The all-glass façades of the world's newest skyscrapers changing the face of cities like New York and Hong Kong could be described by a sixteenth-century man as "swamps of crystal."

59. An unheard of hurricane, raging over two continents . . . I was led in spirit to the great cities on England's east coast. I saw ships thrown on shore, many collapsed buildings, and much wreckage floating on water. At sea many ships were wrecked.

60. Then I was shown Holland, Belgium, and the German coast of the North Sea, which all were heavily visited [by storm and flood]. Among the most afflicted cities I heard the names of Antwerp and Hamburg mentioned. . . . Even Denmark's western and northern coast and Sweden's western coast had suffered.

ANTON JOHANSSON (1918)

61. Hurricane warning systems may be called for as far north as Oslo or Vladivostok.

JOHN HOGUE (1989)

62. From now on tidal waves and cyclones will cause enormous destruction.

CHEIRO (1931)
Cheiro's World Predictions

63. Hurricanes of great violence will afflict not only America, but also Europe, especially England. I saw not less than five great hurricanes.

64. Thunderstorms too will in those years be devastating and will occur in Denmark, North Germany, and southern Sweden.

ANTON JOHANSSON (1918)

65. The destruction of a major southern U.S. metropolitan area [such as Miami or New Orleans] by a global warming enhanced superhurricane will take place in one of the first five hurricane seasons of the new millennium.

JOHN HOGUE (1998)

66. The day of the Lord cometh, because it is nigh at hand. A day of darkness, and of gloominess, a day of clouds and whirlwinds.

JOEL (c. 600 b.c.) *Joel 2:1*

67. The leveling of a major U.S. city by globally warmed storms will galvanize the American people to bring their resources together to fight global warming, as Americans fifty years earlier united to fight Hitler and Japan during World War II.

JOHN HOGUE (1996)

THE GREAT GLOBAL DROUGHT

In a world where the polluted atmosphere traps the sun's heat, extreme weather is the norm. Some areas will be flooded and whipped by dreadful storms, while other regions suffer droughts of biblical proportions. Add to this the dwindling supply of fresh water to sustain a billion new people appearing on the earth in the first eleven years of the new millennium, and the following prophecies will perhaps find their fulfillment.

68. At the 48th degree of the climacteric, [at] the end of Cancer [late July], there is a very great drought.

NOSTRADAMUS (1555) *C5 Q98*

Latitude 48 crosses most of the major grain-producing areas of the world in North America, Europe, and Asia.

69. Mars, Mercury, and the Moon in conjunction [which will take place again in the summer of the year 2000] toward the Midi [southern France and perhaps Africa as well] there will be a great drought.

Nostradamus (1555) *C3 Q3*

70. The waters of the Nile shall drain away, the river shall be parched and run dry: its channels shall stink, the streams of Egypt shall be parched and dry up. The reeds and rushes will wither, also the plants along the Nile, at the mouth of the river [the Nile Delta].

71. Every sown field along the Nile will become parched, will blow away and be no more. The fishermen will groan and lament. Those who throw nets on the water will pine away.

Isaiah (738–687 b.c.) *Isa. 19:5–8*

72. Little rain, hot winds, wars and raids. . . . Bushels of wheat will rise so high that man will devour his fellow man.

Nostradamus (1555) *C4 Q67, C2 Q75*

73. Near the bear [Canis Major constellation] and near the white wool [the Milky Way], Aries, Taurus, Cancer, Leo, Virgo [perhaps for a period of five months], Mars, Jupiter, and the Sun will burn the great plain, woods, and cities.

Nostradamus (1555) *C6 Q35*

The three planets (Mars, Jupiter, and the sun) will be together in Aries in April 2011. We could expect a major drought across the grain belts of the Northern Hemisphere from March through September of that year.

74. Fish in the sea, river and lake boiled hectic, Bearn and Biggore [southwest France] in distress from fire in the sky.

NOSTRADAMUS (1557) *C5 Q98*

75. Blood, earth, plague, hunger, fire, maddened by thirst.

NOSTRADAMUS (1557) *C6 Q10*

THE OCEANS WILL RISE BECAUSE OF GLOBAL WARMING

Increasing global temperatures will precipitate a rise in sea levels of 1.4 to 2.2 meters (4.7 to more than 7 feet) by the end of the twenty-first century. If the Ross Ice Shelf in Antarctica should slip into the oceans as a part of the massive melting of the poles, estimates are that sea levels could rise as much as 16 to 20 feet. The ice shelf could lurch into the southern oceans at any moment.

76. The balance of nature will be lost, when the ocean tides shall obey no shore.

QUETZALCOATL (a.d. 947)

77. Waters Will Overflow.

MADAME SYLVIA (1948),
VIENNESE SEERESS

78. The sea will heave itself beyond its bounds engulfing mighty cities.

BRIGHAM YOUNG (1860)

79. On Earth the nations will be in anguish and perplexity and confusion at the roaring of the sea.

JESUS CHRIST (a.d. 30–33)

Luke 21:25

80. [After the advent of] the great Comet [perhaps Halley's Comet in 1986 or 2062 or Hale-Bopp in 1997] . . . the great nation [clearly described as America in her predictions] will be devastated by earthquakes, storms, and great waves of water, causing much want and plagues.

81. The ocean will also flood many other countries, so that all coastal cities will live in fear, with many destroyed.

HILDEGARD VON BINGEN (C. 1141)

82. Their great city [Paris?] will be greatly damaged by water.

NOSTRADAMUS (1555) C2 Q54

83. The earth will shake, seas will overflow their banks.

EMELDA SCOCHY (1933)

84. And when the seas rise . . . every soul will know what it hath made ready [for the Judgment Day].

MUHAMMAD (a.d. 620–30)

Qur'an 81:12, 14

85. I saw a land swallowed up by the sea and buried with water. But, afterwards, I saw that the sea retreated little by little and the land could be seen again. The tops of the towers in the city rose again above the water and appeared more beautiful than before, and I was told that this land was England.

BALTHASSAR MAS

(SEVENTEENTH CENTURY)

A NEW ICE AGE

Preliminary findings in climatology pose the frightening possibility that an ice age could come as a result of global warming, creating an increased cloud layer that reflects sunlight back into space. The sudden melting of the Antarctic ice could chill the southern oceans and trigger an ice age. New evidence from ice and sea-bottom samples indicates that the previous ice ages could have overtaken the planet in as little as twenty to thirty years, rather than gradually over centuries as was first believed.

86. The end of the world is nigh—yet men are hard and cruel, and listen not to the doom that is coming. Now follows the Age of Northern Winds.

> ANCIENT NORSE PROPHECY
> The Ragnarök

87. A new ridge or belt of land will appear in the North Atlantic which will so cause the Gulf Stream to alter its course that the Eastern States of America will become subjected to intensely cold winters, and the Glacial Age will by degrees be repeated in Northern Europe.

88. These submarine [earthquake] upheavals in their turn affect the great ocean currents and consequently the Gulf Stream, which is of the most vital importance to such countries as Iceland, Ireland, Great Britain, Norway, Sweden, Germany, France, and Spain. Without the warming flow of the Gulf Stream, such countries would quickly become covered with ice, and all vegetation would cease.

> CHEIRO (1931)
> Cheiro's World Predictions

89. Fimbul Winter now comes. All over the world, the heavens are filled with falling snows, and the ground is covered with killing frost. The sun is dimmed, it offers no gladness, while never-ending storms blow and devour the crops.

The Ragnarök

90. The glacial Age will by degrees be repeated in Northern Europe; such countries as Ireland, Great Britain, Sweden, Norway, Denmark, the north parts of Russia, Germany, France and Spain will gradually become uninhabitable.

91. This alteration [the new ice age] will be compensated for by the development of a temperate climate affecting such countries as China, India, Africa, and Egypt, and in consequence a rapid increase of civilization will be the result in all these countries.

CHEIRO (1931)
Cheiro's World Predictions

92. The poor shall now most wisdom know,
And water, wind, where corn doth grow;
Great houses stand with far-flung vale,
All covered o'er with snow and hail.

MOTHER SHIPTON (C. 1561)

93. Harsh winters will come, with record cold at places.

MADAME SYLVIA (1931)

94. The earth and air will freeze a very great water [the Great Lakes?], when they come to venerate Thursday [Thanksgiving Day]: that which will be, never was it so fair [democracy], from the four quarters they will come to honor it [America].

NOSTRADAMUS (1555) C10 Q71

○ ○ ○ ○ ○ ○

EARTH CHANGES

○ ○ ○ ○ ○ ○

There are a family of prophecies dealing with volcanic and seismic catastrophes that alter the map of the globe.

GENERAL CHANGES

95. Natural catastrophes will occur in many parts of the world, and a turbulent activity will begin within the womb of the earth. Great tremors of earth and vehement eruptions of volcanoes will afflict the world and partly also such regions which hitherto have been spared.

ANTON JOHANSSON (1918)

96. The great nation in the [Atlantic] ocean that is inhabited by people of different tribes and nationalities will be laid waste by an earthquake, a storm, and tidal wave. It will be split apart and much of it submerged.

HILDEGARD VON BINGEN (C. 1141)

97. Water and fire will cause terrible earthquakes which will engulf mountains and cities.

PROPHECY OF LA SALETTE (1846)

98. Where water is now there will be land, and where there is land today, wild, swirling water will rush in, destroying everything in its path.

JEANE DIXON (C. 1970S)

99. Darkness and trouble in the air, on the sky and land, when the infidel calls upon God and the Saints.

NOSTRADAMUS (1557) *C9 Q83*

EARTHQUAKES

100. Must also the elements be the instrument of Thy wrath? Enough, O Lord, enough! The cities are wiped out, the natural elements are set loose, the earth quakes in every region.

PROPHECY OF PREMOL (FIFTH CENTURY)

101. Water and fire will cause terrible earthquakes which will engulf mountains and cities.

PROPHECY OF LA SALETTE (1846)

102. The Sun in 20 degrees Taurus [May 10]. There will be a great earthquake. The great theater full up will be ruined.

NOSTRADAMUS (1557) *C9 Q83*

103. New York will suffer a vast earthquake first before Los Angles experiences "the big one"—the long awaited super quake.

VARIOUS PROPHETS

(LATE 20ᵀᴴ CENTURY)

104. Drowsy with peace, war will awaken, the abyss of the temple [of the Vatican] ripped open at Easter [spring 2000?].

NOSTRADAMUS (1557) *C9 Q31*

105. A great kingdom will remain desolate, near the Ebro [Catalan region of Spain] they will be gathered in assemblies. The Pyrenees mountains will console him when in May [spring 2000] there are great earthquakes.

NOSTRADAMUS (1555) *C6 Q88*

106. [By 2031] This upheaval of the ocean bed will break the Isthmus of Panama, North and South America will become two immense islands, and enormous trade will develop through this route.

107. Eastern cities of North America such as Washington, New York, Buffalo, Boston, and Toronto will be seriously affected [by severe earth tremors, reawakening volcanoes, tidal waves and cyclones] and a considerable part of New York will be destroyed.

108. Violent cyclones, with severe earthquakes will occur [in and around Australia] during the coming years, and some unusual phenomenon of nature is indicated.

109. New Zealand [like Australia] will come under similar conditions, with increased danger from earthquakes, storms and tidal waves, especially in relation to [its] Northern Island.

CHEIRO (1931)
Cheiro's World Predictions

110. The earth will speak to us through fire, earthquakes tornadoes and climatic changes.

DR. ADAM CUTHAND (C. 1979),
CREE NATION,
SASKATCHEWAN, CANADA

111. The earth trembles, lifted into the air, placed on the land, Egypt quakes.

NOSTRADAMUS (1555) *C2 Q86*

112. You will hear of magnificent cities, now idolized by the people, sinking in the earth, entombing the inhabitants.

BRIGHAM YOUNG (D. 1877)

113. Earth shaking fire from the center of the Earth will cause the towers around the New City to shake. Two great rocks will war for a long time, and then Arethusa [goddess of volcanic lava] shall color a new river red.

NOSTRADAMUS (1555) *C1 Q87*

114. The earth will tremble and you yourselves will also quake. . . Tremble! The Lord is on the point of delivering you into the hands of your enemies.

PROPHECY OF LA SALETTE (1846)

VOLCANIC ERUPTIONS

115. In Italy [the volcanic eruptions] will be more destructive than ever. Great many people there will save only the clothing on their bare backs. There will be a new eruption of the Vesuvius.

ANTON JOHANSSON (1918)

116. The highest window for seismic and volcanic activity on the West Coast, in New York City, and in St. Louis will be spring of 2000.

VARIOUS PROPHETS

117. Mt. Rainier, Washington, will be vulnerable to a major rock slide or volcanic eruption in the spring of 2000. In the worst-case scenario, a rock slide or a major eruption could send a wall of superheated mud down the river systems that could still be 50 feet high when it reaches the Puget Sound, over fifty miles from the mountain. A wave of superheated mud could threaten downtown Tacoma, Washington, and its dockyards.

JOHN HOGUE (1995)

REDISCOVERY OF THE LOST CONTINENT OF ATLANTIS

If earth changes destine lands to sink into the oceans, others that sank before may rise above sea level. Atlantis, the legendary Atlantic island civilization that is said to have sunk in one terrible night twelve thousand years ago, may rise again. Either it will physically come forth or oceanographers will find objective evidence of submerged Atlantean ruins in the twenty-first century.

118. During the next fifty to a hundred years [1931–2031] after a series of devastating earthquakes, the islands of the Azores will rise from the Atlantic and the ruins of the long lost continent of Atlantis will be discovered and explored.

119. The reappearance of Atlantis [by 2031] will . . . cause the Sahara Desert to be transformed into a huge inland sea and so cause such climatic changes on the continent of Africa that the present arid wastes of the Northern parts of that country, together with Egypt, will be transformed into a temperate zone of such richness that Palestine, Egypt, and the surrounding countries will become the granaries of the world and will make of this portion of the globe a great center of civilization.

CHEIRO (1931)

Cheiro's World Predictions

120. Evidences of this lost civilization are to be found in the Pyrenees and Morocco on the one hand. British Honduras, Yucatán, and America upon the other . . . especially, or notably, in Bimini and the Gulf Stream.

EDGAR CAYCE (1932) *No. 364–3*

○ ○ ○ ○ ○ ○

POLE SHIFT

○ ○ ○ ○ ○ ○

PRELUDE TO THE AXIS SHIFT

Depending on whom you speak to among earth-changes inter-preters of Edgar Cayce, the events mentioned below either should have happened before 1998 or they will begin after 1998.

121. As the equilibrium of the center of the globe becomes altered, great earthquakes will take place in all parts of the world until the Earth's crust will again become settled and normal. From now on, severe earth tremors and quakes will affect countries which have been more or less immune from such occurrences. Extinct volcanoes all over the world will become active, while tidal waves and cyclones will cause enormous destruction to property.

CHEIRO (1931)
Cheiro's World Predictions

122. If there are greater activities in the Vesuvius or Pelée [volcanoes],

123. Then the southern coast of California—and the areas between Salt Lake and southern portions of Nevada—may expect, within the three months following the same inundation by the earthquakes.

124. But these are to be more in the Southern than the Northern Hemisphere.

EDGAR CAYCE (1936) *No. 270–35*

125. Toward the south [perhaps meaning southern France and Africa] there will be a great drought. An earthquake will be reported from the bottom of Asia.

NOSTRADAMUS (1555) *C3 Q3*

126. For several nights the earth will shake. . . . Corinth and Ephesus will swim in two seas [be inundated by tidal waves?].

NOSTRADAMUS (1555) *C2 Q52*

127. Trembling of the earth at Mortara, the tin islands of St. George are half sunk [southwestern England sinks].

NOSTRADAMUS (1557) *C9 Q31*

128. Seven years before the last day, the sea shall submerge Eirin [Ireland] in one inundation.

ST. COLUMBCILLE (a.d. 522)

129. The earth will be broken up. . . . The upper portion of Europe will be changed as in the twinkling of an eye.

130. The greater portion of Japan must go into the sea.

131. The earth will be broken up in the western portion of America.

EDGAR CAYCE (1934) *No. 3976–15*

132. In the next few years lands will appear in the Atlantic as well as in the Pacific.

EDGAR CAYCE (1941) *No. 152–11*

133. The Sun in 20 degrees Taurus [May 10], there will be a great earthquake. The great theater full up will be ruined. Darkness and trouble in the air, on the sky and land, when the infidel calls upon God and the Saints.

NOSTRADAMUS (1557) *C9 Q83*

THE EARTH TURNS OVER

134. There will be omens in the spring, and extraordinary changes thereafter, reversals of Nations and mighty earthquakes. . . . And there shall be in the month of October a great movement of the Globe, and it will be such that one will think the Earth has lost its natural gravitational movement and that it will be plunged into the abyss of perpetual darkness.

NOSTRADAMUS (1557)

Epistle to Henry II, Les Propheties

135. The present world [the fourth to rise out of previous cataclysms] and its sun will end within the present epoch through the advent of dreadful global earthquakes and a cataclysmic finale.

ANCIENT TOLTEC PROPHECY

136. A pair of cosmic giants keep the earth spinning on its correct axis. On the day of the end of the current fourth world [present times], the giants will heed the call of the great spirit and abandon their posts, letting the axis of the Earth fall out of control.

HOPI PROPHECY

137. The shift will have its warnings. Days, years, or decades before the world rolls over on its side, look for the first premonitions of what is to come when the weather becomes increasingly violent, with heavy snowfalls, strong gales, and increased humidity.

JOHN HOGUE, INTERPRETING THE SPIRIT
GUIDES OF RUTH MONTGOMERY

138. After the violence of global weather rises to a new level of apocalyptic fury, for days and nights beforehand the Earth will seem to rock gently, as if soothing a child in its crib.

JOHN HOGUE, INTERPRETING THE SPIRIT
GUIDES OF RUTH MONTGOMERY

139. Now, at the appointed time, the Midgard serpent [who encircles the earth and seas in Norse lore] is shaken with tremendous rage. It trembles and quakes on the Ocean's slimy floor, so violently that its motions cause waves to sweep across the . . . Earth, as high as the mountains. . . . At the same time, the world's mountains shake and the rocks tremble. . . . Mortal men . . . are killed in great numbers, and their shades crowd the path to *Hel* [the Viking underworld]. The sky begins to stretch, and finally breaks in half.

The Ragnarök

140. The world is without support. The heart of the world is broken. . . . The Earth breathes, whirls around in terrible catastrophes. Continents crumble and are washed away, but other continents and islands appear again.

MADAME SYLVIA (1948)

141. The earth reels like a drunkard, it sways like a hut in the wind: so heavy upon it is the guilt of its rebellion that it falls— never to rise again.

ISAIAH (738–687 b.c.) *Isa. 24:20*

142. And there were voices, and thunders, and lightnings; and there was a great earthquake, such as was not seen since men were upon the earth.

ST. JOHN OF PATMOS (a.d. 81–96)
Rev. 16:18

143. In the nighttime areas, the stars will seem to swing giddily in the heavens, and as dawn breaks the sun will seemingly rise from the wrong place on the horizon. In daylight areas, the sun will seem to stand still overhead, and then race backward for the brief period while the Earth settles into its new position relative to the sun.

144. Those who are capable of reaching safety will see the Earth's surface tremble, shudder and in some places become a sea of boiling water, as the oceans pour upon the land. Simultaneous explosions beneath the Earth's crust will bring new land above the surface of the waters, as other areas are swallowed by the sea.

SPIRIT GUIDES OF RUTH MONTGOMERY
(1979) Strangers Among Us

145. So mighty an earthquake, and so great and the great city [Jerusalem] was divided into three parts, and the cities of the nations fell.

ST. JOHN OF PATMOS (a.d. 81–96)
Rev. 16:18–19

146. We ask that you picture a giant wave, higher than a ten-story building, racing toward shore. Impossible to escape it, so in that moment of terror it is well to put aside fear and think only of the good that is to come by passing into spirit.

SPIRIT GUIDES OF RUTH MONTGOMERY
(1979) Strangers Among Us

147. And every island fled away, and the mountains were not found.

ST. JOHN OF PATMOS (a.d. 81–96)
Rev. 16:20

148. The Earth will be like a vast cemetery. Corpses of the impious and the just will cover it. The Earth will tremble to its foundations, then great waves will agitate the sea and invade the continents.

MARIE JULIE (1880)

149. By the gigantic changes and upheavals thus created [by the alteration of the Earth's axis] bring about such alterations in climate that "tropical" parts become "temperate" and "temperate" change to "tropical" in the course of time.

CHEIRO (1931)

Cheiro's World Predictions

150. Many people will not survive this shift, but others will, because after a period of churning seas and frightful wind velocities the turbulence will cease, and those in the north will live in a tropical clime, and vice versa.

RUTH MONTGOMERY (1971),

CHANNELING ARTHUR FORD

A World Beyond

151. When the Earth is shaken with her violent quaking, and the Earth brings forth her burdens, and man says: What has befallen her? On that day she shall tell her news, because your Lord had inspired her. On that day men shall come forth in sundry bodies that they may be shown their works. So, he who has done an atom's weight of good shall see it. And he who has done an atom's weight of evil shall see it.

MUHAMMAD (a.d. 620–30)

Qur'an 99

152. Yet now, when all seems lost, miraculously a new dawn has come. The sun shines bright again. . . . Earth rises a second time from the sea, clad with green pastures and forests—a thing of beauty to behold. The morning air is filled with the sounds of falling waters.

The Ragnarök

"Falling waters" could refer to the seas falling after the curtailment of global warming in the next century, or it may indicate the end of floods after the axis shift around 2000–2012.

153. Prophets tend to exaggerate. Perhaps the emotional impact of their visions tends to make their declarations unbalanced. With this in mind, I predict that the earthquakes and land changes generally foreseen will not at all be as serious as predicted. Certainly there will be land changes. In the Great Alaskan Quake of 1964, the land was thrust up 50 feet here and sank 50 feet there along the Alaskan coast. Certainly there will be 8 or even 8.5 earthquakes on the seismic scale that could level many a famous city in the coming period of seismic activity scheduled around the spring of 2000—2008; however, I predict the earth-changes prophecies of doomsayers like Dolores Cannon and Gordon Michael Scallion will be discredited. There will *not* be a sinking of the western United States in 2000 or for the next two thousand centuries! If I'm wrong, I'll eat Nostradamus's hat!

154. I predict that some people who took Gordon Michael Scallion's advice and moved out of California because he predicted it would sink into the ocean will demand that he pay the expenses for their return.

JOHN HOGUE (1997)

GEOGRAPHY IN THE POST-MONTGOMERIAN WORLD

155. In the 1970s and 1980s, Ruth Montgomery's spirit guides adamantly forewarned their medium, the former Washington, D.C., reporter, that a shift of the earth's axis would take place sometime after 1998. They said it was not possible to target the exact degree of the slide, but they did intimate that the future North Pole would rest in the Pacific and the South Pole would move to somewhere in South America.

Using their guidance, one can draw a map that children of the third millennium will study in class. For the new South Pole to align itself close to the southern part of South America without the North Pole missing the Pacific completely, a shift of 40 degrees in a northeasterly direction is required. This slides the new South Pole from its current position to a spot just north of Uruguay, next to the Brazilian city of Porto Alegre. That puts the North Pole several hundred miles east of Tokyo.

> *What has not been described by her guides is just what kind of climate and geography would be left after such a catastrophic shift. Here's what I predict the world would look like if—and I repeat, if—her discarnate spiritual augurs have got it right:*

156. If Montgomery's guides have seen the future correctly, what is left of Japan after quakes and inundations will be enclosed in a tomb of ice. The Pacific shorelines of New Guinea, Indonesia, the Philippines, and East Asia should experience weather similar to that of today's Arctic Alaskan and Siberian coastlines.

157. The East China and South China seas might remain locked in ice floes for centuries. Some of the most densely populated regions of Asia would quick-freeze in a sudden axis shift. Billions of Asians might share the same fate as herds of mammoths did in the last big tilt; hundreds of thousands of years hence, archaeologists will find them in a final freeze-dried tableau caused by the sudden roll of the earth over on its side.

158. The same would be the fate of millions of South Americans living from São Paolo to Buenos Aires, stretching west to the snaggletoothed wall of the Andes. Balmy Rio de Janeiro would turn into a frigid Nome, Alaska, almost overnight.

159. The turbulence and climatic chaos following an axis shift would dump a massive snowfall on the Andes, giving birth to a mile-high glacial wall. This would slide eastward from Patagonia in the south all the way to northern Peru, grinding and burying most of Argentina, Paraguay, Bolivia, and half of Brazil under a blanket of mountainous ice. With time, what had not been destroyed of the Amazon rain forest would become Antarctic pine forests and tundra. The Amazon River might exchange its yellow-red flood of silt for gray glacial runoff.

160. The former Arctic regions would undergo an equally drastic change for the hotter. Antarctica would emerge from its coat of ice as a large archipelago, tracing its former outline in chains of islands; most of its land mass will already have sunk beneath the sea level because of the weight of its mile-high ice shelves. By the next millennium, the once frigid and inaccessible continent would gather about itself coral reefs and sandy white beaches. What were sterile gray islands would find themselves wrapped in a sarong of palm trees and rain forests, rivaling the once tropical (but now subarctic) islands of Tahiti and Bora Bora. The icy graveyard of Scott's Antarctic expedition would become the next tropical paradise.

161. In the next few thousand years most of the Antarctic land mass now free of its icy burden would creep above sea level.

162. With time, another new tropical heaven would grow around the Hudson Bay. The Canadian Arctic outposts of Fort Reliant and Fort Churchill could become as sultry as present-day Singapore.

163. The first week after a "Montgomerian" shift, the Eskimo nation of Greenland would see the island's ice shelf slush itself out of existence down new cataracts along the rocky and mountainous coastline. Nature would finally correct Viking explorer Erik the Red's famous misnomer: the future "green land" might become a tropical island outline of its former self, a vast atoll surrounding thousands of square miles of lagoon.

164. One would find the Arabian desert transforming itself into a dense Amazonian jungle.

165. Poland would look more like Paraguay.

166. Central Europe and the western approaches of Russia could end up covered by rain forest.

167. The Rocky Mountains in former North (now equatorial) America might resemble the present-day Andes mountains of a future (Antarctic) South America. The former east-facing slope of the Rockies would be covered with rain forests stretching southeast across what once was North America's greenhouse-dried fields of grain. New monsoon patterns would make the Mississippi rival the once proud tropical flood of the Amazon.

168. If Ruth Montgomery's spirits are right, the Australians who survive the ultimate eco-disaster will have to drop saying they come from "down under," since the Australasian continent would find itself at the current latitude of the United States. Perth, Sydney, and Melbourne will exchange their cold and wet westerly storms coming off the southern seas at wintertime for an annual summer deluge—the gift of a newly created monsoon pattern similar to the one that floods Mumbai (Bombay) every June through September.

169. Central Africa will become as temperate as Kansas.

170. Senegal and Zaire will welcome the English weather,

171. While the entire eastern seaboard from Ethiopia to Durban, South Africa, will become subtropical to tropical.

172. Temperate Central Asia will be the next breadbasket of the world.

173. The once inhospitable tundra fields and Arctic forests of Northern Canada and Siberia would become mostly tropical, opening large areas of virgin land for future civilizations to build their resorts and get their suntans on beaches overlooking the warm waters of the equatorial (Arctic) ocean.

JOHN HOGUE (1989)

○ ○ ○ ○ ○ ○

DEEP IMPACT FROM OUTER SPACE

○ ○ ○ ○ ○ ○

Prophets centuries ago may have seen what only recently science has acknowledged: that there is a clear and present danger that a comet or meteorite will collide with the earth. It is no longer an issue of "if," but "when." Whether it happens tomorrow or a thousand years from now, the following prophecies may give us hints of what a cosmic collision might do.

DATING THE EVENT: IS IT IN THE NEAR FUTURE?

174. Before the comet comes, many nations, the good included, will be scourged by want and famine.

HILDEGARD VON BINGEN (C. 1141)

175. God will send two punishments; one will be in the form of wars, revolutions and other evils; it shall originate on earth. The other will be sent from Heaven. There shall come over the whole earth an intense darkness lasting three days and three nights. Nothing can be seen, and the air will be laden with a pestilence which will claim mainly, but not only, the enemies of religion. It will be impossible to use any man-made lighting during this darkness, except blessed candles. He, who out of curiosity, opens his window to look out, or leaves his home, will fall dead on the spot. During these three days, people should remain in their homes, pray to Rosary and beg God for mercy.

ANNA-MARIA TAIGI (1835)

176. By its tremendous impact the comet will force much water out of the ocean and flood many countries, causing much want and many plagues. All coastal cities will live in fear, and many of them will be destroyed by tidal waves, and most living creatures will be killed, and even those who escape will die from horrible diseases. For in none of those cities does a person live according to the laws of God.

HILDEGARD VON BINGEN (C. 1141)

A MOUNTAIN FALLS FROM THE SKY

177. The great mountain, one mile in circumference, after peace, war, famine, flooding . . . It will spread far, drowning great countries. Even antiquities and their mighty foundations.

NOSTRADAMUS (1555) *C1 Q69*

178. At the place where Jason has his ship built [the Aegean coast of Greece], there will be such a great sudden flood that one will not have a place or a land to fall on. The waters rise over the Olympic Festulan.

NOSTRADAMUS (1557) *C8 Q16*

> The last sentence may refer to Mt. Olympus, just under 10,000 feet in elevation, and/or the city of Fresole in Tuscany, just under 1,000 feet above sea level, and describe what the initial impact of a meteor or comet 1 mile in circumference would do: throw a wall of sea water over 10,000 feet, unleashing tsunamis large enough to run seventy-five miles up Italy's Arno Valley and crest at 900 feet above sea level.

179. Because of heat like that of the sun upon the sea, the fish around Negrepont [modern-day Evvoia, Greece, where Jason built his ship] will become half cooked.

NOSTRADAMUS (1555) *C2 Q3*

180. With blood and famine [perhaps again hinting at the coming apocalypse] even greater calamity: seven times it [tidal waves from the impact?] approaches the seashore of Monaco.

NOSTRADAMUS (1557) *C3 Q10*

181. The city is almost burned down by fire from the sky, water again threatens Deucalion [the Greek name for Noah].

NOSTRADAMUS (1555) *C2 Q81*

SAFE AREAS

182. [Virginia Beach] will be among the safety lands as will be portions of what is now Ohio, Indiana, and Illinois and much of the southern portion of Canada, and the eastern portion of Canada; while the western land, much of that is to be disturbed—in this land [western North America]—as of course, much in other lands.

EDGAR CAYCE (1941) *No. 1152–11*

183. Lowlands of Europe are in a perilous situation, continue her guides, but larger land masses away from the sea such as in Canada, Russia, Siberia, Africa, and China will be relatively safe.

SPIRIT GUIDES OF RUTH MONTGOMERY

(1979) Strangers Among Us

184. The Holocaust is not going to be confined to certain places, it is going to be global so no escape will be possible. You can only escape within and that's what I teach. I do not teach worship of God or any other ritual, but only a scientific way of coming to your innermost core.

OSHO (1983)

Noah's Ark of Consciousness Declaration

○ ○ ○ ○ ○ ○

PLAGUES

○ ○ ○ ○ ○

The biblical prophets pinpoint the final years before the second millennium as the time we begin to see the seven pestilential scourges appear all over the earth.

THE SEVEN PLAGUES OF THE TWENTY-FIRST CENTURY

185. And I saw another sign in heaven, great and marvelous, seven angels having the seven last plagues; for in them is filled up the wrath of God.

ST. JOHN OF PATMOS (a.d. 81–96)

Rev. 15:1

186. And the seven angels came out of the temple, having the seven plagues, clothed in pure and white linen, and having their breasts girded with golden girdles. And one of the four beasts gave unto the seven angels seven golden vials full of the wrath of God, who liveth for ever and ever. And the temple was filled with smoke from the glory of God, and from his power; and no man was able to enter into the temple, till the seven plagues of the seven angels were fulfilled.

ST. JOHN OF PATMOS (a.d. 81–96)
Rev. 15:6–8

187. Simultaneously with these trials by nature [earthquakes, volcanic eruptions, and more violent hurricanes], great epidemics will roam about the world, carrying off many victims.

188. [Epidemics] will be more dangerous than all others and will spread over the whole world, claiming an immense number of victims.

ANTON JOHANSSON (1918)

THE FIRST PLAGUE: A BLOOD PESTILENCE (AIDS? EBOLA?)

189. The first [angel] went, and poured out his vial upon the earth; and there fell a noisome and grievous sore upon the men which had the mark of the beast, and upon them which worshipped his image.

ST. JOHN OF PATMOS (a.d. 81–96)
Rev. 16:2

190. Saturn joined with Scorpio [transiting] Sagittarius at its highest ascendant: Plague . . . The century as well as the age draws close to its renewal.

> NOSTRADAMUS (1555)
>
> C1 Q16

This astrological transit took place in the autumn of 1985—the year the AIDS epidemic became mainstream news around the world.

191. In the meantime [there appears] so vast a plague that two-thirds of the world will fail and decay. So many die that no one will know the true owners of fields and houses, and there will be a complete desolation of the Clergy.

> NOSTRADAMUS (1557)
>
> Epistle to Henry II

A plague that specifically attacks the Catholic priesthood could imply that sexual contact among men spreads the disease in a community of backsliding celibate priests.

192. Swords [the occult symbol for the phallus] damp with blood from distant lands. A very great plague will come with a great scab. Relief near but the remedies far away.

> NOSTRADAMUS (1555)
>
> C3 Q75

193. Those at ease will be suddenly cast down. . . . Hunger, fire, *blood*, plague, and all evils doubled.

> NOSTRADAMUS (1555) C8 Q17

194. In Lucca [Italy] it will come to rain *blood* and milk. Shortly before the change of governor: Great plague and war, famine and drought will be seen.

NOSTRADAMUS (1555) *C3 Q19*

AIDS is called "Slim" in Africa, because its attack on the body makes the victims look like they are dying of famine.

195. In the meantime [there appears] so vast a plague that . . . there will be a complete desolation of the [Roman Catholic] Clergy.

NOSTRADAMUS (1557)

Epistle to Henry II

The purported homosexual practices of some monks and priests in the church may act as the vector for AIDS in the clergy.

196. Mostly the [epidemics] will be a serious pulmonary disease, but there will be also other unknown maladies, one such that people will become utterly emaciated, another one similar to leprosy, because the flesh of the afflicted persons will start to peel off.

ANTON JOHANSSON (1918)

THE SECOND PLAGUE: THE OCEAN PESTILENCE

197. The second angel poured out his bowl on the sea, and it turned into blood like that of a dead man, and every living thing in the sea died.

> ST. JOHN OF PATMOS (a.d. 81–96)
> *Rev. 16:3*

198. These are the Signs that great destruction is coming. . . . You will hear of the sea turning black [oil spills?], and many living things dying because of it.

> WHITE FEATHER (1958),
> HOPI BEAR CLAN
> *Recorded by Rev. David Young*

THE THIRD PLAGUE: THE RADIATION PESTILENCE IN FRESH WATERS

199. The third angel poured out his bowl on the rivers and springs of water, and they became blood.

> ST. JOHN OF PATMOS (a.d. 81–96)
> *Rev. 16:4*

200. And the third angel sounded, and there fell a great star from heaven, burning as it were a lamp, and it fell upon the third part of the rivers, and upon the fountains of waters; and the name of the star is called Wormwood: and the third part of the waters became wormwood [bitter]; and many men died of the waters, because they were made bitter.

ST. JOHN OF PATMOS (a.d. 81–96)
Rev. 8:10–11

Wormwood in Ukrainian is "Chernobyl." The radiation fallout from this nuclear disaster in 1986 covered a third of the land masses of the planet.

201. The first twenty-five years of the twenty-first century will see a major nuclear power plant disaster in the United States.

LINUS PAULING (1976)

202. In the Cyclades, in Perinthus and Larissa, in Sparta and all of the Peleponnesus [the southern Balkans and Greece]: a very great famine, plague through false dust [fallout?].

NOSTRADAMUS (1555) *C5 Q90*

203. Then there will be no bread for people anymore and no fodder for animals.

204. Poisonous clouds, manufactured by human hands, will sink down and exterminate everything. The human mind will be seized by insanity.

PROPHECY OF MARIA LAACH
MONASTERY (SIXTEENTH CENTURY)

THE FOURTH PLAGUE: THE OZONE HOLE PESTILENCE

205. And the fourth angel poured out his vial upon the sun; and power was given unto him to scorch men with fire. And men were scorched with great heat, and blasphemed the name of God, which hath power over these plagues; and they repented not to [glorify] him.

> St. John of Patmos (a.d. 81–96)
>
> *Rev. 16:8–9*

206. The first blow of the sword of God, which will fall like lightning on humanity. The mountains and all nature will tremble because of the disorder and the misdeeds of men, which will rise to the very heavens.

> Prophecy of La Salette (1846)

207. There will be poisonous clouds and rays which can burn more deeply than the equatorial sun.

> Prophecy of Warsaw (1790)

208. A great change will come to pass, such as no mortal man will have expected.

> Pastor Bartholomaeus
>
> Holzhauser (c. 1642)

209. There will be planes shaped like pencils that will take men into space and by so doing punch holes in the atmosphere, letting in lethal cosmic rays that will kill many millions.

> Emma Kunz (1938)

210. Heaven and Hell will confront each other is this struggle. Old states will perish and light and darkness will be pitted against each other with swords, but it will be swords of a different fashion. With these swords it will be possible to cut up the skies and to split the Earth. A great lament will come over all mankind and only a small batch will survive the tempest, the pestilence and the horror.

PASTOR BARTHOLOMAEUS
HOLZHAUSER (C. 1642)

211. At first will come several terrestrial scourges, as great wars [World Wars I, II, and perhaps III?], through which many millions will run into destruction.

After that will come the celestial scourge in full severity, such as has never been. It will be short, but will cut off the greatest part of mankind.

MARIA TAIGI (1835)

212. If the world community postpones serious efforts to replenish the ozone layer, expect an ozone hole to appear over the Arctic between 2020 and 2030. It will be as large as the one currently hovering over Antarctica. The hole will appear in early spring and last until late September every year. It will cover North America, Europe, and northern Russia. People in these regions will have to wear force-30 sunscreen, cover up, and wear sunglasses during the spring and summer months. By 2040 the intensity of the ultraviolet light will seriously burn unprotected skin after exposure for only one hour.

JOHN HOGUE (1999)

THE FIFTH PLAGUE: DEPRESSION, HOPELESSNESS

213. Man is becoming mature and aware that he has been cheated by the false promises of the priests and politicians. Society has been feeding him on false hopes. The day he matures and realizes this, the desire to live falls apart. And the first thing wounded by it will be your sexuality. To me that is AIDS! AIDS has nothing to do either with homosexuality or heterosexuality; to me it means humanity is simply losing its will to live. Whenever a person loses the will to live, his resistance falls immediately, because the body follows the mind. The body is a very conservative servant of the mind. If the mind loses the will to live, it will be reflected in the body by the dropping of resistance against sickness, against death.

OSHO (1985)

From Darkness to Light

214. The fifth angel poured out his bowl on the throne of the beast, and his kingdom was plunged into darkness. Men gnawed their tongues in agony and cursed the God of heaven because of their pains and their sores, but they refused to repent.

ST. JOHN OF PATMOS (a.d. 81–96)

Rev. 16:10–11

215. And modern man has finally come to a point where he finds that the life he is living is meaningless. He suddenly feels that he's an existential orphan, and this feeling causes his will to live to disappear.

OSHO (1985)

From Darkness to Light

THE SIXTH PLAGUE: THE PESTILENCE OF FALSE PROPHETS

216. The sixth angel poured out his bowl on the great river Euphrates, and its water was dried up to prepare the way for the kings from the East. Then I saw three unclean spirits that looked like frogs; they came out of the mouth of the dragon, out of the mouth of the beast and out of the mouth of the false prophet. They are spirits of demons performing miraculous signs, and they go out to the kings of the whole world, to gather them for the battle on the great day of God Almighty.

ST. JOHN OF PATMOS (a.d. 81–96)

Rev. 16:12–14

217. A short time before the king is murdered, Castor and Pollux [John Paul I] and the ship [a clue for the papacy] . . . A bearded star [Halley's Comet, 1986]. Public treasure emptied on land and sea.

NOSTRADAMUS (1555) *C2 Q15*

Journalists exposed the Vatican Bank scandal in 1986 exactly at the time the Halley's Comet transited the skies.

218. Then the impurities and abominations will be brought to the surface and made manifest . . . toward the end of a change in reign [perhaps the end of the cycle of centuries in the year 2000?].

219. The leaders of the Church will be backwards in their love of God. . . . Of the three sects the Catholic is thrown into decadence by the partisan differences of its worshipers. The Protestants will be entirely undone in all of Europe and part of Africa by the Islamics, by means of the poor in spirit who, led by a madman [a terrorist], shall through worldly luxury [oil, consumerism, and drugs?] commit adultery.

NOSTRADAMUS (1557)
Epistle to Henry II

220. O great Rome, your ruin draws near. Not of your walls but of your blood and substance: the harsh one of letters will make so horrid a notch, pointed steel all wounding up the sleeve.

NOSTRADAMUS (1557) *C10 Q65*

In 1986, reports claimed that the Vatican Bank was a front used by underworld sources to launder millions of dollars of drug money. In other words, Nostradamus could be describing the pointed steel of drug addicts' syringes making needle tracks up their arms.

221. But mercy, mercy for Rome! But Thou hearest not my entreaties, and Rome also collapses in turmoil. And I see the King of Rome with his Cross and his tiara, shaking the dust off his shoes, and hastening in his flight to other shores. Thy Church, O Lord, is torn apart by her own children. One camp is faithful to the fleeing Pontiff, the other is subject to the new government of Rome which has broken the Tiara.

PROPHECY OF PREMOL (FIFTH CENTURY)

222. Someday a pope will flee from Rome in the company of only four cardinals . . . and they will come to [Cologne].

HELEN WALLRAFF (NINETEENTH
CENTURY)

THE SEVENTH PLAGUE: HUMAN EVIL

223.　The seventh angel poured out his bowl into the air, and out of the temple came a loud voice from the throne, saying, "It is done!" Then there came flashes of lightning, rumblings, peals of thunder and a severe earthquake. No earthquake like it has ever occurred since man has been on Earth, so tremendous was the quake. The great city [Jerusalem] split into three parts, and the cities of nations collapsed.

St. John of Patmos (a.d. 81–96)
Rev. 16:17–19

224.　Many will say to me on that day [Judgment Day], "Lord, Lord, did we not prophesy in your name, and in your name drive out demons and perform many miracles?" Then I will tell them plainly, "I never knew you. Away from me, you evildoers!"

Jesus Christ (a.d. 30–33) *Matt. 7:22*

225.　God remembered Babylon the Great and gave her the cup filled with the wine of the fury of his wrath.

St. John of Patmos (a.d. 81–96)
Rev. 16:19

226.　From the sky huge hailstones of about a hundred pounds each fell upon men. And they cursed God on account of the plague of hail, because the plague was so terrible.

St. John of Patmos (a.d. 81–96)
Rev. 16:21

227.　Because of the evil deeds of the land the ground is parched, no rain has fallen upon it.

Jeremiah (587 b.c.) *Jer. 14:4*

228. In Russia the [plagues] will be especially intense, and the voice told me that these and other diseases would visit Russia because of her great impiety. If I remember correctly, a fourth part of her people will perish through these diseases. One of the most dangerous diseases will consist of people becoming blind and losing their mind. For those afflicted by this disease, it will be very dangerous to drink alcohol.

ANTON JOHANSSON (1918)

229. Mankind will be decimated by epidemics, famine, and poison. . . . Only few will be left to rebuild the world. The future is approaching at a quick pace.

SEERESS REGINA (EARLY TWENTIETH CENTURY)

230. Merlin saith that in England shall be seen many strange things . . . great hunger among the people, great oppression of blood.

MERLIN (FIFTH CENTURY)

231. This is the plague with which the Lord will strike all the nations that fought against Jerusalem: Their flesh will rot while they are still standing on their feet, their eyes will rot in their sockets, and their tongues will rot in their mouths.

ZECHARIAH (C. 160 b.c.) *Zech.* 14:12

UV plagues from the skies might be behind Zechariah's prediction of eyes rotting in their sockets, in other words, pandemic cataracts. The depletion of the ozone layer could be the source of the biblical plagues of "ulcers and sores" many will suffer from widespread skin cancer brought on by stronger doses of daily solar radiation.

232. The human being has abused all the holy connections and he has created total disharmony. If no change is happening, if his understanding about its meaning is not getting transformed from its roots, he will throw himself into the abyss of disaster. Nothing of what you see around you is contradicting this.

AMBRES (1986)

○ ○ ○ ○ ○ ○

Y2K AND OTHER FORMS OF SUPERSYSTEM COLLAPSE

○ ○ ○ ○ ○ ○

In his book The Coming Dark Age, *futurist Roberto Vacca posits that our modern civilization's survival depends on what he calls supersystems—superorganizations sustained by machines and single energy sources. The collapse of any one of these interdependent global systems—such as information retrieval, telecommunications, medicine, transportation, or global agricultural production and distribution—could have a domino effect on all the other systems.*

Y2K IS A WARNING OF GREATER SUPERSYSTEM CHALLENGES TO COME

When the calendar flips over from 1999 to the year 2000, sensitive computer chips that monitor records, file your taxes, balance your bank drafts, pump your gasoline, direct your air liner to the airport strip, pump your sewage, pump your fresh water, keep the city lights on, and do a thousand-plus other things will read "00"—or "uh, oh!"—in their little electric brains and either think it's 1900 or blanche in cybershock. In either case they could all shut down, unless programmers can replace the chips or fix the software in time.

233. There is something positive about things coming unglued. The danger of supersystem collapse may bring people all over the world together to prevent it. The Y2K problem is the first of several challenges we will face in the next thirty years. It is a dress rehearsal for much larger global problems coming in 2010, when the fossil-fuel reserves begin to collapse, and then ten years later, when food and water reserves could collapse from population strains. What we learn from the coming Y2K crisis could help us avoid greater dangers to our global supersytems.

JOHN HOGUE (1998)
CBS's Unsolved Mysteries

234. Soon the Earth will shake and will tumble down and people will say, "Oh my God! Oh my God!" But the Great Spirit will say, "They're not praying to me, they're saying, 'All my Gold! All my Gold!'" This is how it will be.

WALLACE BLACK ELK (1985),
LAKOTA SIOUX NATION

235. The cities will be plagued with blackouts, pollution, growing unemployment, and soaring crime.

DR. ADAM CUTHAND (C. 1979),
CREE NATION,
SASKATCHEWAN, CANADA

236. In the midst of the land lie the old world-cities, empty receptacles of an extinguished soul. . . . Men live from hand to mouth, with petty thrifts and petty fortunes, and endure.

OSWALD SPENGLER (1926)
The Decline of the West

THE COMING COLLAPSE OF FOSSIL-FUEL RESERVES

237. *L. F. Ivanhoe, president of Novum Corporation, an international energy-exploration consulting firm, is a geologist, geophysicist, engineer, and oceanographer. He has more than a half century of domestic and international experience in petroleum exploration with a number of private and government oil companies. Suffice it to say that he is no lightweight in the oil business. Ivanhoe dropped a bombshell in his article in the January-February 1997 issue of the* Futurist *warning that consumption of oil is outstripping the supply and the discovery of new fields. He says that the numbers popularly advertised by politicians and oil corporations indicating that there are enough reserves for another half century of high levels of consumption are generally fudged. Ivanhoe believes we are heading for a sudden and permanent drop in oil reserves as early as 2010.*

238. I would add that by the 2010s the only large and relatively untapped oil reserves left will bring added political clout to Russia, China, and Iraq.

JOHN HOGUE (1998)

239. Current consumption of the Earth's resources will see them exhausted by 2072.

EUROPEAN FUTURISTS OF THE CLUB OF ROME (1972)

240. After oil ceases to flow, the plastics industry will go down, no more new computers, telephone lines, nylon clothing or winter heating oil. Then the tractors harvesting food will stop running. The trains and trucks shipping wheat to the cities will dwindle. Next the supersystem of law enforcement would be overwhelmed by food riots, even in America. Without fuel, world commerce would grind to a standstill. No jets would fly, no ships would carry their cargoes. Finally, governments would collapse, and revolutions and dictators abound.

JOHN HOGUE (1994)

A COLLAPSE OF FRESH-WATER AND FOOD SUSTAINABILITY

Nostradamus, the biblical prophets, and others forewarn of a close relationship between the coming final war and global famine.

241. The world's ability to feed its growing numbers will completely collapse by 2072.

242. Current pollution of the Earth's environment collapse no later than 2072.

EUROPEAN FUTURISTS OF THE CLUB OF
ROME (1972)

243. In 1972, the Hopi elder Rolling Thunder said that white men should stop trying to teach red Indians Christianity and should begin to listen to what the "Great Spirit taught" the Hopis. If they opened their minds and hearts to the Hopi wisdom, they could bring the earth back in harmony with nature. "As it is, the white man is destroying his country," concluded Rolling Thunder.

JOHN HOGUE, INTERPRETING ROLLING
THUNDER (1972)

TOO MANY PEOPLE, NOT ENOUGH JOBS AND RESOURCES

Currently unemployment in western Europe is at an all-time high with over twenty million European workers facing the new millennium without work. One of the most serious side effects of adding a billion people to the planet every eleven years in the first half of the twenty-first century will be finding them all jobs.

244. The global economy collapses, in 2072, never to recover.

EUROPEAN FUTURISTS OF THE CLUB OF
ROME (1972)

245. Unless we control our population and find new energy sources, the global civilization will break down between 2009 and 2039.

ISAAC ASIMOV (1979), SCIENCE FICTION
WRITER AND FUTURIST

246. By the year 2072, overpopulation will cause the civilization to collapse.

EUROPEAN FUTURISTS OF THE CLUB OF
ROME (1972)

247. After the great clearance, during which pestilence will tarry in the air and in the cellars and on the roof, millions of men will have no free ground anymore, no country and no home, because many cities will be no more and the frontiers of many states will be fixed anew.

STORMBERGER (EIGHTEENTH CENTURY)

248. The birth of babies malformed by chemicals will hasten the stampede back to the land and the simple life of our forefathers. Once again, we will learn to be self-reliant. Once more we will attend to our spiritual welfare.

DR. ADAM CUTHAND (C. 1979),
CREE NATION,
SASKATCHEWAN, CANADA

SUPERSYSTEM BREAKDOWN CAUSES THE NEXT WORLD WAR

249. World War III started tomorrow because the postman didn't ring twice. Didn't ring at all. The ICBMs came down because the toilets backed up, the phone didn't work, and your bank went on vacation—forever.

Sound ludicrous? This is only the tip of the iceberg. How ironic it would be if Armageddon came because the electricity was cut off. What if all the prophetic threats of nuclear terrorism and every warning of doomsday around the year 2000 proved to be full of hot air—and still World War III happened because the grain trucks never came into town?

JOHN HOGUE (1994)
The Millennium Book of Prophecy

World War from Lack of Drinking Water

Over 40 percent of the world's six billion people depend on 214 major river systems shared by two or more countries for irrigation, hydropower, or just a life-sustaining drink. Fresh water disputes in the Middle East in another thirty years could bring on a war that no peace agreement could prevent.

250. And the sixth angel poured out his vial upon the great river Euphrates; and the water thereof was dried up, that the way of the kings of the east [those destined to fight Israel in the battle of Armageddon] might be prepared.

ST. JOHN OF PATMOS (A.D. 81–96)
Rev. 16:12

251. Mars, Mercury, and the Moon in conjunction [2 July and 1 August 2000]. Toward the South [the Southern bloc?], there will be great drought. . . . Both Corinth [Greece] and Ephesus [Turkey] will then be in a troubled state.

NOSTRADAMUS (1555) C3 Q3

252. In the year Saturn and Mars are equally fiery [1997 or 1998 and several more times between 2000 and 2030], the air is very dry, a long meteor [missile?]. From hidden fires a great place burns with heat. Little rain, hot wind, wars and raids.

NOSTRADAMUS (1555) C4 Q67

253. It said to the sixth angel who had the trumpet, "Release the four angels who are bound at the great river Euphrates." And the four angels who had been kept ready for this very hour and day and month and year were released to kill a third of mankind.

ST. JOHN OF PATMOS (a.d. 81–96)
Rev. 9:14–15

World War from Hunger

254. Sometime in the early twenty-first century, the North American grain belts might be blowing away in dust devils when global warming pushes the right climate for grain growing into the tundra fields of Canada. The grain-harvesting equipment, barns, and empty grain elevators of America and Canada could become hosts for gathering sand dunes. By the 2020s America's grain reserves will have run out. The former food superpower will be forced to cut off all exports. One hundred countries will begin to starve. In Africa in the next two years five hundred million people will die. Since the beginning of the decade, a hundred governments began watching their social machinery break down. The world holds its breath as Russia, with thirty-five hundred nuclear weapons remaining after START (Strategic Arms Reduction Treaties), disintegrates into a pack of military dictatorships fighting over what's left of the food.

JOHN HOGUE (1990)

255. After a great misery for mankind an even greater approaches when the great cycle of the centuries is renewed [A.D. 2000]. It will rain blood . . . famine, war.

NOSTRADAMUS (1555) C2 Q46

256. The world may boycott America in the future, just as Iraq was isolated in the 1990s, not because it is harboring weapons of mass destruction, but because it is dragging its feet in curtailing its serious pollution of the world.

JOHN HOGUE (1999)

257. By the 2020s or 2030s, if America ceased exporting grain because of its own food crisis, hundreds of cities in the world would go hungry. It has been estimated that entire continents could starve if America didn't or couldn't resume grain exports. In two years over a half a billion Africans would starve to death.

258. By the 2020s or 2030s China might go to war with America over an embargo of American grain exports.

JOHN HOGUE (1990)

259. They will destroy each other, caring not for the blood and lives of their neighbors, of their families, or of their own lives. Famine will spread over the nations, and nation will rise against nation, kingdom against kingdom, and states against states, in our own country [America] and in foreign lands.

BRIGHAM YOUNG (1860)

260. The Battles of the past will be only skirmishes compared to the battles that will take place . . . [because of general] Famine and pestilence . . .

ST. ODILE (a.d. 720)

○ ○ ○ ○ ○ ○

ARMAGEDDON

○ ○ ○ ○ ○ ○

Armageddon is the scene of a final battle between the forces of good and evil prophesied by the Bible to occur at the end of the world. Biblical prophets expect it will take place near the town of Megiddo, site of numerous battles in the Old Testament.

261. When pictures look alive with movements free,
When ships like fishes swim beneath the sea,
When men outstripping birds can soar the sky,
Then half the world, deep drenched in blood, shall die.

MOTHER SHIPTON (C. 1561)

WARFARE IN THE FUTURE

262. The ancient peoples have left behind witnesses of inner silence, radiance, benediction, and beauty, and nations of the future will only pass on traces of plague and death. Every new generation develops weapons of destruction more horrible than before. This development you cannot stop, because they have become slaves of their own fear.

ATTRIBUTED TO NOSTRADAMUS
(C. 1564)

263. The place of the permanent armies as we know them will gradually be taken by professional forces of volunteer war-keen soldiers; and from millions we shall revert to hundreds of thousands.

OSWALD SPENGLER (1926)
The Decline of the West

264. All manmade progress will be enlisted for destruction.

Manuscript (1888) from Montreal, Canada

265. Russia is devising an electronic system that will be able to knock out U.S. communications at the press of a button. Communication with orbiting satellites could then be lost, and the U.S. thereby shut off from quick information and powerless to respond if a surprise attack should be launched at that time.

SPIRIT GUIDES OF RUTH MONTGOMERY
(1985) Aliens Among Us

Ruth Montgomery's channeled spirit guides, Edgar Cayce, and other seers noted for their high percentage of accuracy use the term "Russia," rather than "the Soviet Union." Before the remarkable events of 1991, interpreters might have excused this variation as a matter of semantics. Perhaps the best prophets have always foreseen that the Soviet Union had no future and now Russia has inherited the electromagnetic gun?

266. Evil spirits of air will call forth strange things upon the Earth and will throw men into destruction.

PROPHECY OF LA SALETTE (1846)

267. There will be let loose living fire and hidden death, horror inside dreadful globes. The city on fire, helpful to the enemy.

NOSTRADAMUS (1555) *C5 Q8*

268. "Swords" of subjective "steel" are unsheathed from their scabbards of fiber-optic cable. The "swoosh" of arrows in the New Age pulse the atmosphere with the static of their electromagnetic passage. Tomorrow's doomsday warriors need not launch nuclear weapons to fight World War III. They can release their attack by computer keyboard.

269. No roar of a rocket engine heralds doomsday, but the click of a mouse. Rather than releasing biological weaponry, one enemy can disrupt the technology of another with a virtual plague of computer viruses, shutting down all communication and radar equipment.

270. A logic bomb can crash a country's air-traffic control system and reroute its railroad trains into collisions.

271. Imagine you are seeing your president suddenly begin to make unpopular changes in his policy, alienating him from his people. Has he gone mad, or has the enemy jammed the TV signals and replaced his image with a computer-morphed replica?

272. According to *The Day After . . . in Cyberspace*, a Rand Corporation war game played in 1995 by senior U.S. officials (first reviewed by *Time* magazine [21 August 1995]), the early twenty-first century may see the first global infowar. The Pentagon's Defense Science Board conceded that any Third World nation with enough computer software know-how could "procure a formidable, modern information-warfare capability virtually off-the-shelf."

> JOHN HOGUE (1997) The Millennium
> Book of Prophecy, *2d ed.*

273. Smart bullets will be the rifle munitions of First World armies by 2020. They will have electronic eyes that seek out their enemy like large cruise missiles seek out their targets.

274. By 2020 tanks will be made obsolete by smart missiles and bullets.

275. The United States will use antimatter protons to enhance its smaller nuclear arsenal, reduced to a few thousand bombs by the START. The United States will try to retain its might with more "quality" weapons of mass destruction rather than quantity. By the 2030s there will be antimatter thermonuclear devices that will be a hundred thousand times more destructive than the Hiroshima blast.

John Hogue (1999)

THE THIRD WORLD'S WAR IN THE 2020S

> *The Cold War is over, but the next global conflict can still sneak up on us if the means to feed, clothe, and light the developing nations breaks down from overpopulation, ecological disaster, and epidemic "dis-ease."*

276. Hearken, hearken to what will transpire in the latter days of the world! There will be great wars.

St. Columba of Ireland
(sixth century)

277. In the second period will be peace [1945–2020s?], but only by name, not in reality. The tribulations will be as great as during a war. . . . God will pour out the spirit of deception over them, and they will want what they don't want, will not want what they do want, and their actions will become so preposterous that they will not be able to do what they are able to do. At noonday they will grope about like in darkness.

PASTOR BARTHOLOMAEUS
HOLZHAUSER (C. 1642)

278. And after the second great struggle between the nations will come a third universal conflagration, which will determine everything. There will be entirely new weapons. In one day more men will die than in all previous wars combined. Battles will be fought with artificial guns [lasers, radar beams?].

STORMBERGER (EIGHTEENTH CENTURY)

279. At the onset of the last crisis in the Persian Gulf, Native American medicine men were deeply concerned that former U.S. president George Bush might launch air attacks on Iraqi munitions plants. Their spokesman, James Fry, director of the Elders Survival Fund, an adjunct to the Teton Treaty Council in Pine Ridge, South Dakota, sent a world communiqué about the prophetic nightmare Native Americans on the council collectively foresaw. They envisioned U.S. jets bombing factories in Iraq in an air attack that would *release clouds of death that will circle and devastate the entire planet.* Fry added that these clouds would consist of *chemical or biological weapons that the United States doesn't know anything about.*

If there is a Gulf War III, the Native Americans may still see their cloud of botulism, anthrax, and nerve gas agents spread over the earth. Disturbing revelations in late 1996 concerning the Gulf War Syndrome have added more weight to the dire plague prophecy of the Teton Treaty Council. The mysterious and debilitating illnesses suffered by Gulf War veterans could be sexually transmitted to the general public. Apparently the men and women exposed to biological and chemical agents on the battlefields of Kuwait may be carrying genetically altered microorganisms in their bioplasma, or bodily fluids. These microorganisms have even been found deep within the nuclei of cells, where they may be altering the way cells talk to each other on a genetic level. New surveys show that 77 percent of the spouses of Gulf War veterans and 66 percent of their children have similar symptoms of rashes and an assortment of immunological disorders. After sexual contact, many wives and girlfriends of male veterans describe how the semen burns "like battery acid" when it touches their skin. Some doctors are advising couples to practice safe sex and use condoms. No one knows yet whether these mutated microorganisms can be transmitted by more casual contact through saliva and sweat. At present the Pentagon is not confirming these new findings until more research is done.

> JOHN HOGUE (1997), INTERPRETING THE
> GRAND TETON COUNCIL PROPHECY
> The Millennium Book of Prophecy,
> *2d ed.*

280. A horrible war which is being prepared in the West, the following year the pestilence will come, so very horrible that young nor old, nor animal [may survive]. Blood, fire, Mercury, Mars, Jupiter in France.

> NOSTRADAMUS (1557) *C9 Q55*

The next conjunctions of Jupiter, Mars, and Mercury are 2004, February 2009 (in Aquarius), April-May 2011 (in Aries, its closest conjunction to the Mayan calendar's date for the end of time as we know it, in 2012), and December 2011 through January 2020 in Capricorn.

281. The pestilence that might trigger the war could then come in several forms: as a biological weapon that unleashes a global plague, a nuclear disaster, ozone depletion, a plague of genetically mutated microbes, or a new and rapid spread of Ebola virus or AIDS.

JOHN HOGUE (1997)

282. Gigantic catastrophes will occur. With open eyes will the nations of the Earth enter into these catastrophes. They shall not be aware of what is happening, and those who will know and tell, will be silenced. Everything will become different than before, and in many places the Earth will be a great cemetery. The third great war will be the end of many nations.

STORMBERGER (EIGHTEENTH CENTURY)

283. It is only War in the end that will save humanity. It is only when the world will be satiated with blood, destruction, and violence that it will wake from its present nightmare of madness—and thus it is that the coming "War of Wars" fits into the design of things.

CHEIRO (1931)
Cheiro's World Predictions

284. The world will be so diminished, and its people will be so few that no one will be willing or in enough numbers to till the fields which will remain wild as long as ever they were tilled.

NOSTRADAMUS (1557)
Epistle to Henry II

285. Many people will want to come to terms with the great world leaders who will bring war upon them. The political leaders will not want to hear anything of their message. Alas! If God does not send peace to the Earth.

NOSTRADAMUS (1561) *C8 Q4 duplicate*

286. While in theory there is nothing which is absolutely inevitable, in actuality there are things which are almost inevitable. People believe that wars happen in the future, whereas in reality they happen in the past; the fighting is only a consequence of many events which have already occurred. Viewed from this perspective, all the causes of the Third World War have already happened. There is therefore only a very remote possibility that the conflict itself will not take place.

OSHO (1985)

The Land of the Lotus Paradise

The Brothers of the North (America and Russia)

Nostradamus is among a minority of prophets who apparently never thought a thermonuclear exchange between the United States and the Soviet Union was likely. Indeed, the third world war may come "after" Russia and America have ended the Cold War and attempted to become allies.

287. One day the two great leaders will become friends: their great power will be seen to increase. The new land [America] will be at the height of its power.

NOSTRADAMUS (1555) *C2 Q89*

This prophecy is numbered quatrain 89 of Century 2 in Nostradamus's book *Les Propheties (The Prophecies)*, implying the year 1989 as the beginning of the end of the Cold War and the turn toward Russo-American friendship.

288. Three years and seven months having passed, they [China and the United States? or Russia and the United States?] will go to war. Their two vassals [allies] rebel against them. The victor is born on American soil.

NOSTRADAMUS (1555) C4 Q95

289. China will eventually lose the war, but only after the United Sates and its allies will have suffered great loss.

HANS HOLZER (1971) Survey of the
Future, from The Prophets Speak

290. And when shall the lords be two in number, victorious in the north against the eastern ones, there shall be a great noise and warlike tumult that all the East shall quake for fear of those two brothers of the North [America and Russia] who are not yet brothers. . . . They will be victorious against the Easterners.

NOSTRADAMUS (1557)
Epistle to Henry II

291. The two [brothers of the North] will not remain allied for long: within thirteen years they give in to Barbary [Libyan-Arab] power. There will be such a loss on both sides, that one will bless the bark of Peter and the cape of the pope.

NOSTRADAMUS (1555) C5 Q78

An alternate reading of the last line is: "That one will bless the bark and the cape of Pope Peter." Pope Peter is the name given by St. Malachy to the last pope before the tribulation and Judgment Day.

292. When the Eastern War appears, know the end is near.

JOANNA SOUTHCOTT (C. 1815)

Political Alliances for World War III

293. In *My Journey with a Mystic,* Fritz Peters relates that his master, George Ivanovich Gurdjieff, a former citizen of czarist Russia, foresaw a day when the Eastern world would again rise to a position of world importance and become a threat to the "momentarily all-powerful, all-influential new culture of the Western world, which was dominated by America"—a country, according to Gurdjieff, that was very strong, though very young.

294. When north shall thus divide the south [division of the rich Northern Hemisphere from the overpopulated and poor Southern Hemisphere];

The eagle built in lion's mouth [America born out of England];

Then tax and blood and cruel war,

Shall come to every humble door.

MOTHER SHIPTON (C. 1561)

295. Within fifty years there will be only three great nations. . . . Then, within fifty years there will be eighteen years of war and cataclysms.

ARGHATI PROPHECY (CENTURIES AGO)

The three great nations may be the First, Second, and Third Worlds formed after the last world war. This prophecy may indicate that their collapse into chaos will begin just prior to 1995. In that year the violence and threatened spread of ethnic wars in the Balkans and Chechnya captured international attention and galvanized international efforts for enforcing peace and stanching the spread of bloody ethnic wars over the earth. The verdict is still out on whether they will be successful.

296. In 1986, peace will once again reign, yet it will last only a few years.

PROPHECY OF WARSAW (1790)

297. Those at ease will suddenly be cast down. The world put into trouble by three brothers. Famine, fire, flood, plague, all evils doubled.

NOSTRADAMUS (1557) *C8 Q17*

298. Strifes will arise through the period. Watch for them near the Davis Strait in the attempts there for the keeping of the lifeline to land open. Watch for them in Libya and Egypt, in Ankara [Turkey] and in Syria, through the straits about those areas above Australia; in the Indian Ocean and the Persian Gulf.

EDGAR CAYCE (1941) *No. 3976–26*

The Davis Strait is between Canada and Greenland. The land therefore is most likely Russia, to which aid is being shipped from America. By abandoning communism, Russia is rapidly fulfilling collective prophecies that place it as America's ally in the coming third world war to be fought mainly over Palestine. Cayce may be warning us to watch for terrorists or political adventurers based in Libya, Egypt, and Syria who might be preparing for that war of Armageddon. Cayce clearly specifies the West's major oil shipping lanes and the Persian Gulf as vulnerable future targets.

299. As foreshadowed in Ezekiel, Chapter 38, the great battle of Armageddon will be fought on the plains of Palestine. It is clearly set out for all those who may choose to read that this conflict will be a life and death struggle for the contending armies fighting in Palestine. It describes that the people of the North, by which Russia is evidently indicated . . . will descend into that country "with allies drawn from Persia [Iran], Ethiopia, Libya and many people."

CHEIRO (1931)
Cheiro's World Predictions

300. The United States will fight China, and Russia will be allied to the United States. Europe will also be affected by war, several [European Union] nations joining in alliance with the United States and Russia. China will dominate the entire East, and important battles will take place in the Middle East.

HANS HOLZER (1971) *Survey of the*
Future, from The Prophets Speak

301. What a great oppression shall be made upon the princes and governors of kingdoms and. . . especially those that shall live eastward and near the sea [the Mideast and North Africa]. Their language intermixed with all nations. The language of the Latin nations [southern Europe] mixed with Arabic and North African communication.

NOSTRADAMUS (1557)
Epistle to Henry II

302. There shall come the Son of Man, having a fierce beast in his arms, whose kingdom lies in the Land of the Moon [the crescent of Islam in the Middle East and North Africa], which is dreadful throughout the whole world.

MOTHER SHIPTON (C. 1561)

Next we see the Arab triumvirate and its eastern ally, China, suffer the mother of all massacres through the overwhelming firepower of the great Northern powers sometime in our near future.

303. All the Eastern Kings shall be driven away, beaten and brought to nothing, not only because of the strength of the Northern Kings just before the new age [2000], but also by means [or by the fault] of three secretly united [Iran, Libya, and Syria?], seeking for death by ambushes [terrorism?] one against the other. The renewing of the triumvirate shall last seven years [1999–2007?].

NOSTRADAMUS (1557)

Epistle to Henry II

Acts of Terrorism Trigger the War

304. The sky will burn at [latitude] 45 degrees. Fire approaches the great new City. In an instant a huge scattered flame leaps up.

NOSTRADAMUS (1555) *C6 Q97*

On the 45th latitude are New York, Paris, and Belgrade, making them key targets for a terrorist attack. Past terrorist attempts in New York make it the most likely target; however, the NATO bombing of Belgrade in the Kosovo War of 1999 may also be implied.

305. I [Allah] will cast terror into the hearts of those who disbelieve.

Therefore strike off their hands and strike off every fingertip of them.

MUHAMMAD (a.d. 620–30) Qur'an 8:12

Just as Christian fundamentalists could misinterpret the book of Revelation as instruction to blow things up, so could Islamic fundamentalists misconstrue Muhammad's message from Allah and start a third world war.

306. The plague of false dust [fallout?] will last nine months through the whole peninsula [Italy] as of Peleponnesus [Greece].

NOSTRADAMUS (1557) *C5 Q90*

Nostradamus interpreters believe this refers to either a nuclear plant disaster when Y2K shuts down any number of faulty eastern European nuclear reactors, or a cloud from a biological or nuclear attack by terrorists.

307. There will be poisonous clouds . . . [and] flying vessels full of terrible bombs and arrows.

PROPHECY OF WARSAW (1790)

308. Poisonous clouds, made by human hands, will sink down and exterminate everything. The human mind will be seized by insanity.

PROPHECY OF MARIA LAACH
MONASTERY (SIXTEENTH CENTURY)

309. Europe will be completely covered with a yellow fog that will kill the cattle in the fields. Those nations which began the war . . . will perish by terrible fire. May the Lord grant my grandchildren the grace of perseverance in the coming hard times.

> FRANCESCA DE BILLANTE OF SAVOY
> (EARLY TWENTIETH CENTURY)

Their Target? Israel! Their Goal? A Second Holocaust!

310. For a long time there will be disharmony in the Mideast, until at last Israel faces up to the terrible truth that it is not always right and others always wrong. They have been termed the Chosen People, but are they more chosen than those who themselves choose God? . . . It would be ridiculous to say that the Mideast crisis will pass until the hearts of men are uplifted. The smoldering fire remains until man himself alters his consciousness and overcomes hatred and greed.

> SPIRIT GUIDES OF RUTH MONTGOMERY
> (1971) A World Beyond

311. Right-wing fundamentalist rabbis successfully wage an overthrow of secular government in Israel sometime after 2005.

312. Arabs launch a chemical and biological attack on Israel with great lost of life. Israel counterattacks with nuclear weapons.

313. America will be hard-pressed to support a fundamentally extremist and undemocratic Israeli government, yet it will not abandon its ally, Israel, during her climactic great war in the early twenty-first century.

MODERN JEWISH CABALISTIC SEERS

314. The word of the Lord came to me: ". . . In that day, when my people Israel are living in safety . . . you [Gog of the land of Magog] will come from your place in the far north, you and many nations with you."

EZEKIEL (C. 593–571 B.C.) *Ezek. 38:1, 14–15*

"When my people Israel are living in safety": Perhaps this means that any apparent resolution of the Palestinian homeland questions is a precursor to Armageddon. Gog and Magog could stand for the allied coalition attacking Iraq, or Syria, or someone of their ilk.

315. At the same time when Gog shall come against the land of Israel . . . there shall be a great shaking in the land . . . and all the men that are upon the face of the Earth shall shake at my presence . . . and every wall shall fall to the ground. . . .

On that day I will give Gog a burial place in Israel, in the valley of those who travel east toward the Sea. It will block the way of travelers, because Gog and all his hordes will be buried there. So it will be called the Valley of Hamon Gog.

EZEKIEL (C. 593–571 B.C.)

Ezek. 38:18–20; 39:11

Here's a biblical link to Nostradamus: according to him, Baal Hammon is the Antichrist's God. Ancients worshiped this Phoenician deity in the regions of present-day Syria, Libya, and Iraq, implying the source of Israel's enemies. In his destructive mood, Baal Hammon is known as the terrible lord of the skies. Nostradamus, in C10 Q72 of his book *Les Propheties*, predicts that a King of Terror will descend from the skies in July of 1999. This terror could be a thermonuclear war escalating from a war in the Middle East at that time, or it stands for an incident in the Middle East that will initiate the twenty-seven-year war of Nostradamus's Third Antichrist.

316. Alas, how we will see a great nation [Israel?] sorely troubled and the holy law in utter ruin. Christianity governed throughout by other laws, when a new source of gold and silver is discovered [oil?].

NOSTRADAMUS (1555) *C1 Q53*

317. On that day men will be stricken by the Lord with great panic. Each man will seize the hand of another, and they will attack each other.

ZECHARIAH (C. 160 B.C.) *Zech. 14:13*

318. But your many enemies will become like fine dust, the ruthless hordes like blown chaff. Suddenly, in an instant, the Lord Almighty will come with thunder and earthquake and great noise, with windstorm and tempest and flames of a devouring fire. Then all the hordes of all the nations that fight against Ariel [situated in the currently disputed West Bank], that attack her and her fortress and besiege her, will be as it is with a dream,. . .

319. As when a thirsty man dreams that he is drinking, but he awakens faint, with his thirst unquenched [an allusion to water running out in the Mideast?]. So will it be with all the hordes of all the nations that fight against Mount Zion.

ISAIAH (738–637 B.C.) *Isa. 29:5–8*

320. A new law will occupy a new land around Syria, Judea, and Palestine: The great empire of the [Arab] barbarian will crumble before the Century of the Sun is finished.

NOSTRADAMUS (1555) *C3 Q97*

321. There will be a time of distress such as has not happened from the beginning of nations until then. But at that time your people [Israel] . . . will be delivered.

DANIEL

(SIXTH–FOURTH CENTURIES b.c.)

Dan. 12:1

Submarines in the Mediterranean Sea Attack the European Union

322. When the fleet travels under water.

NOSTRADAMUS (1555) *C3 Q13*

323. From the East will come a dreadful act which will strike at the Adriatic sea and the heirs of Romulus [Italy]. With the Libyan fleet, the inhabitants of Malta and its archipelago tremble with fear.

NOSTRADAMUS (1555) *C1 Q9*

This could be another reference to a submarine being used in a nuclear terrorist attack on Italy's shores.

324. When weapons and plans are enclosed in a fish [a submarine]—when Mars and Mercury are in conjunction with Pisces—out will come a man who will then make war. His fleet will have traveled far across the sea to appear at the Italian shore.

NOSTRADAMUS (1555) *C2 Q5*

Nostradamus in other predictions makes it clear that there's a Libyan (Barbary) connection to a future (terrorist) invasion of southern Europe. Muammar Qaddafi, an admitted protector and supporter of Abu Nidal and other terrorist organizations, also possess five Soviet-made Foxtrot Class diesel-powered attack submarines in his fleet. Algeria and Egypt also have small submarine fleets. Whoever the man who has plans and special weapons to "make war" is, he may borrow a North African submarine.

325. Through lightning in the box [ark] gold and silver are melded. The two captives will devour each other. The greatest one of the city stretched when the fleet travels under water.

NOSTRADAMUS (1555) *C3 Q13*

The first two lines could be a description of an alchemical process or a six-teenth-century man's attempt to describe the function of a modern subma-rine's atomic engines.

326. By night the city [Rome] will be reduced to dust by the [submarine] fleet.

NOSTRADAMUS (1555) *C5 Q8*

327. During the appearance of the bearded star [Comet Hale-Bopp in 1997, or a new comet?]. The three great princes will be made enemies [future American, Russian, and Chinese leaders?]. The shaky peace on earth shall be struck from the skies: the Po, the winding Tiber, a serpent [weapon?] placed on the shore.

NOSTRADAMUS (1555) *C2 Q4*

Terrorist commandos can attack Europe with a weapon of mass destruction, perhaps a bio-plague. It is transported to the mouth of the Tiber River, where they follow the river up to the city of Rome. The attack on Rome triggers a world war.

328. From the useless enterprise of honor and undue complaint, the ships [submarines?] are tossed upon the sea off the Italian coast. Not far from the Tiber river where the land is stained with blood. There will be several plagues upon mankind.

NOSTRADAMUS (1556) *C6 Q63*

329. Naples, Palerma, and all of Sicily will be uninhabited through North African [Libyan] hands. Corsica, Salerno, the island of Sardinia—hunger, plague, war.

NOSTRADAMUS (1556) *C7 Q6*

330. From Monaco as far as Sicily, all the coast will remain deserted.

NOSTRADAMUS (1555) *C2 Q4*

331. Paterno will hear the cry from Sicily. . . . Flee, oh flee . . . the dreaded pestilence!

NOSTRADAMUS (1557) *C8 Q84*

A Fleet in the Persian Gulf Melted and Sunk?

The old millennium ends with U.S. carrier fleets on almost permanent patrol in the Arabian Sea and the Persian Gulf. An attack by either Saddam Hussein using atomic mines or missiles or Iran using nuclear torpedoes shot from its new submarine fleet could sink a U.S. fleet in the waters around the Arabian peninsula.

332. The Punic [Libyan] treachery broken in the East, Great Jordan and Rhône, Loire, and Tagus will change: When the he-mule will be satiated. Fleet sprinkled, blood and bodies will swim.

NOSTRADAMUS (1555) C2 Q60

This prophecy may date the events of submarine attacks in southern Europe and the sinking of a Western fleet in the waters surrounding Saudi Arabia at the time that a U.S. president of the Democratic party, represented by the mule, is in power.

333. In the Arabian Gulf a great fleet will flounder.

NOSTRADAMUS (1555) C6 Q44

334. One will see blood rain upon the rocks. The sun [atomic bomb?] in the East. Saturn [the Grim Reaper] in the West.

NOSTRADAMUS (1555) C5 Q62

335. War near Orgon [southern France], a great evil seen near Rome [the submarine terrorist attack mentioned earlier]. The ships melted and sunk by the Trident [missile].

NOSTRADAMUS (1555) C5 Q62

The Twenty-Seven-Year War of the Third Antichrist (1999–2026)

The war begins either with a terrorist act or as a result of a smoldering war in the Middle East in the summer of 1999. The conflict leads to a larger war either between Israel and its Arab neighbors, a new Gulf War with Iraq, or even a widening conflict in the Kurdish regions of Asia Minor. The war may take years to spread across the world, but it eventually draws in America, Russia, and China. The war is waged primarily by smaller rogue nations of the Southern Hemisphere using weapons of terror against the formidable military and technologically superior northern forces.

336. In 1999 and seven months the great king of terror will come from the sky.

He will bring back to life the king of the Mongols [Ghengis Khan]. Before and after Mars, the God of war [and of transformation], reigns happily.

NOSTRADAMUS (1557) C10 Q72

337. From the kingdom of Fez [North Africa] they will reach out to those of Europe [E.C.]. The city [Paris] blazes, the sword will slash: the great man of Asia [the new Ghengis Khan] by land and sea with a great troop so that blues, perse [Iranians] he will drive out the cross [Christian nations] to death.

NOSTRADAMUS (1556) C6 Q80

An alternate reading of the last line is: "So that Shiites, Iranians, the cross drives out to death."

338. The Antichrist very soon annihilates the three. Twenty-seven years his war will last [1999–2026].

NOSTRADAMUS (1557) C8 Q77

339. A period of peace will follow [the end of the Cold War is implied], but only for the space of twenty-five years [1990–2015?]. The forerunner of the Antichrist will assemble an army of men drawn from many nations united under his banner [Islam or a U.S./E.U. coalition?]. He will lead them in a bloody war against those still faithful to the loving God.

PROPHECY OF LA SALETTE (1846)

Commentators on Nostradamus see two time windows for a twenty-seven-year war of the Antichrist. In the first, the war begins in 1973 and climaxes in 1999. The second starts the countdown with 1999 and ends with Armageddon in 2026.

340. At the time of the end the king of the South [bloc?] will engage him [the Antichrist] in battle, and the king of the North [bloc?] will storm out against him.

> DANIEL
>
> (SIXTH–FOURTH CENTURIES b.c.)
>
> *Dan. 11:40*

341. Important battles will take place in the Middle East. Europe will also be affected by war.

> HANS HOLZER (1971) *Survey of the*
> *Future, from* The Prophets Speak

342. When those of the northern pole are united together, in the East there will be a great fear and dread. A new man elected. . . . Both Rhodes [Greece] and Byzantium [Turkey] will be stained by barbarian [anagram for "Arab" or "Libyan"] blood.

> NOSTRADAMUS (1555) *C6 Q21*

343. He will invade [and] . . . extend his power over many countries: Egypt will not escape. . . . The Libyans and Nubians [Sudan] in submission.

> DANIEL
>
> (SIXTH–FOURTH CENTURIES b.c.)
>
> *Dan. 11:42–43*

344. In his story *The Stolen Bacillus* (1895), science fiction writer and prophet, H.G. Wells foresaw there will come a day when small guerrilla-style groups will steal a deadly bacillus and make random demands.

345. He will set out in a great rage to destroy and annihilate many. . . . Yet he will come to his end and no one will help him [international boycott?].

> DANIEL
> (SIXTH–FOURTH CENTURIES b.c.)
> *Dan. 11:44–45*

346. Nuclear weapons and germ weapons will be used, though only to a limited degree.

> HANS HOLZER (1971) *Survey of the Future, from* The Prophets Speak

347. Smallpox will be the biological weapon of choice of terrorists between the years 1999 and 2026. The organizations will glean the microbes from Russian scientists seeking employment abroad after abandoning the collapsing Russian federation.

> JOHN HOGUE (1999)

348. New York, Chicago, and the West Coast are possible targets for destruction.

> HANS HOLZER (1971) *Survey of the Future, from* The Prophets Speak

349. I saw a wide meadow, over which the sky suddenly reddened. Red rain began to fall. Under it a great number of people died.

> MARIA AND ELSA OF VOLTAGO, ITALY
> (1937)

350. The populated lands will become uninhabitable. Great disagreement in order to obtain lands [the Palestinian question, Kashmir, and the Balkans?]. Kingdoms given to men incapable of prudence. Then for the great brothers [United States and Russia] death and dissension.

NOSTRADAMUS (1555) *C2 Q95*

351. The rule will be left to two [United States and China?]. They will hold it for a very short time. Three years and seven months having passed, they will go to war.

NOSTRADAMUS (1555) *C4 Q95*

352. The years 1998–2000 are a treacherous wicket, as Saturn, Jupiter, Neptune shift signs, as we change car gears. And when they do so shift, it does mean tensions, trials, tiffs, tribulations, tests, and the long, winding trail of blood, gore, and devastation and "resultation" of death, debris, and decay.

BEJAN DARUWALLA (1989)

353. A horrible warrior will unleash it, and his enemies will call him Antichrist. All nations of the Earth will fight each other in this war. The fighters will rise up in the heavens to take the stars and will throw them on cities, to set ablaze the buildings and cause immense devastations. . . . The nations will cry "peace, peace," but there will be no peace.

PROPHECY OF ST. ODILE (a.d. 720)

The Balkanization of the World

A destiny of global war is described here as something like a worldwide rash of civil wars and social breakdown, a

Balkanization of human civilization. Ethnic cleansing is a plague that could infect entire continents by the 2020s, if its spread from regions in the Balkans, Africa, Trans-Caucasia, and the Middle East is not curtailed.

354. The peace among men which will set in after the great scourge [World War II and the Cold War] will be only an ostensible peace. During this period the Earth will shake because of manifold concessions and convulsions. Mankind will experience continuous wars, which finally will lead to the last great war.

PROPHECY OF LA SALETTE (1846)

355. Thou dashest together for me the weapons of war, and with thee I will dash nations together, and with thee I will destroy kingdoms: And with thee I will break in pieces the horse, and his rider, and with thee I will break in pieces the chariot, and him that getteth up into it: and with thee I will break in pieces man and woman and with thee I will break in pieces the old man and the child, and with thee I will break in pieces the young man and the virgin: And with thee I will break in pieces the shepherd and his flock, and with thee I will break in pieces the husbandman and his yoke of oxen, and with thee I will break in pieces captains and rulers. . . . Behold I come against thee, thou destroying mountain, saith the Lord, which corruptest the whole earth; and I will stretch out my hand upon thee, and will roll thee down from the rocks, and will make thee a burnt mountain.

JEREMIAH (C. 580 B.C.) *Jer.* 51:20–23, 25

356. There will be more grievous wars and battles, and there will be towns, cities, chateaux and all other buildings burnt, desolated and destroyed with a great effusion of virgin blood, the raping of married women and widows, and suckling children dashed to pieces against the walls of towns, and so many [other] evils will be committed under the aegis of Satan that infernal Prince, that almost the entire world will be undone and desolate. Before these events [take place] many rare birds [peacemakers or spiritual teachers?] will cry in the air, "Now! Now!" and sometime later will vanish.

NOSTRADAMUS (1557)
Epistle to Henry II

357. Suddenly vengeance will be revealed coming from a hundred hands [nations?].

NOSTRADAMUS (1555)
C2 Q62

358. And the people shall rush one upon another, and every man against his neighbor: the child shall make a tumult against the ancient, and the base against the honorable.

ISAIAH (738–687 b.c.) *Isa. 3:5*

359. Nation will rise against nation, and kingdom against kingdom.

JESUS CHRIST (a.d. 30–33) *Matt. 24:7*

360. There will be perpetual warfare. . . . There will be a terrible war between the Earth's peoples.

ARGHATI PROPHECY (CENTURIES AGO)

361. A war shall follow with the work,
Where dwells the pagan and the Turk.
The States will lock in fiercest strife,
And seek to take each other's life.

MOTHER SHIPTON (C. 1561)

362. Behold, the days come when the inhabitants of earth shall be seized with great panic, and the way of truth shall be hidden, and the land be barren of faith. And iniquity shall be increased above that which thou thyself now seest or that thou hast heard of long ago.

EZRA (587–539 b.c.) *4 Ezra 5:1–2*

363. For with many afflictions shall they be afflicted that inhabit the world in the last times, because they have walked in great pride.

EZRA (587–539 b.c.) *4 Ezra 8:50*

364. When in the world there shall appear quakings of places, tumult of peoples, schemings of nations, confusion of leaders, disquietude of princes, then shalt thou understand that it is of these things the Most High has spoken since the days that were aforetime from the beginning.

EZRA (587–539 b.c.) *4 Ezra 9:3–4*

365. The weaker the world grows through age, so much the more shall evils increase upon the dwellers of the earth. Truth shall withdraw further and falsehood be near at hand.

EZRA (587–539 b.c.) *4 Ezra 14:16–17*

366. Behold, the days come when the Most High is about to deliver them that are upon the earth. And there shall come astonishment of mind upon the dwellers on earth: and they shall plan to war one against another, city against city, place against place, people against people, and kingdom against kingdom.

EZRA (587–539 b.c.) 4 Ezra 13:29–31

367. Nobody will endure his fellow man anymore. Even the Lord, our God, will be dragged out of his corner. Everybody will have his own, different mind. The little ones will become great, the great ones small. Laws will be made that nobody will keep, and taxes announced that nobody will be able to pay.

STORMBERGER (EIGHTEENTH CENTURY)

368. What then will be the condition of that people when this great and terrible [civil] war shall come? It will be very different from the war between the North and South [in America]. . . . It will be a war of neighborhood against neighborhood, city against city, town against town, country against country, state against state, and they will go forth destroying, and being destroyed and manufacturing will, in great measure, cease, for a time, among the American nation. . . .

Their cities will be left desolate. The time is coming when the great and populous city of New York . . . will be left without inhabitants.

ORSON PRATT (1879), MORMON LEADER

369. Financial disasters and ruin of property will cause many tears to fall. . . . Almost the whole world will be turned upside down. Men will be without sanity and without piety.

PROPHECY OF WARSAW (1790)

370. Everywhere there is war! Peoples and nations are pitted against each other. War, war, war! Civil and foreign wars! Mourning and death everywhere! . . . Will [Paris] be destroyed?

PROPHECY OF PREMOL (FIFTH CENTURY)

371. Paris will be destroyed by fire and Marseilles will be flooded by the sea. Other great cities will also be destroyed by fire—razed to the ground by fire.

PROPHECY OF LA SALETTE (1846)

Connecting flaming Paris with a flooded Marseilles may indicate that the Balkanization of the world may result from the chaos caused by oceans rising from global warming.

372. The Gallic Babylon [Paris] will be besieged by iron and fire, and will be brought down by a great conflagration, and inundated with flood. Afterward, other large cities of France will be destroyed.

ST. CAESARIUS OF ARLES (a.d. 470–542)

373. The seven-headed city [Rome], now more admirable than Jerusalem, shall be a place more desolate than Jerusalem.

MEDIEVAL SAXON PROPHECY

374. Moles will be the models for soldiers under the earth to the depth of 300 feet.

MARIENTHAL PROPHECY (1749)

Nuclear warriors fire their missiles in bunkers hundreds of feet deep.

375. There shall be poisonous clouds, and [atomic?] rays which can burn more deeply than the equatorial sun, armies on the march encased in iron, flying ships full of terrible bombs and arrows, and flying stars [future SDI space weapons?] with sulfuric fire which destroy whole cities in an instant.

376. There will come in the year 2000 the day of the Lord, who will judge both the living and the dead. Stars and comets [missiles?] will fall from above, the Earth will be set ablaze with lightning [nuclear flashes or laser beams], and the old Earth will pass away.

PROPHECY OF WARSAW (1790)

377. A single day will see the burial of mankind, all that the long forbearance of fortune has produced, all that has been raised to eminence, all that is famous and all that is beautiful: great thrones, great nations—all will descend into one abyss, all will be overthrown in one hour.

Sibylline Oracles *(second century B.C.)*

378. At sunrise a great fire will be seen. Noise and light extending toward the North. Within the world death and cries are heard, death awaiting them through weapons, fire, and famine.

NOSTRADAMUS (1555) *C2 Q91*

379. Frenzy, folly and madness. . . . Two corpses by the roadside, two fallen colossi [United States and Russia, or United States and China?], terrible struggle, lament, wreck, ruin and smoke. Where is the sun? Where is day? Where is God and his help? Everything is dark on Earth. Hell has opened its gates.

MADAME SYLVIA (1948)

380. Heavy snows are driven and fall from the world's four corners. The murdering frost prevails. The Sun darkened at noon. It sheds no gladness. Devouring tempests bellow and never end. Men wait for the coming of summer in vain. Twice winter follows winter over the world which is snow-smitten, frost-fettered, and chained in ice.

The Ragnarök

Fimbul Winter, the holocaust of ice forewarned by Viking prophets, could take place after the battle of Ragnarök, the Norse version of Armageddon, when dust thrown up from nuclear explosions could block out the sun for months or even years.

381. Immediately after the suffering of those days the sun will be darkened and the moon will not give its light and the stars [atomic warheads?] will fall from the sky and the power of the universe will be shaken [atomic detonations?].

JESUS CHRIST (a.d. 30–33) *Matt. 24:29*

382. A winter will come, darkness for three days, lightning, thunder and cleft in the earth. . . . A poisonous breath will fill the night with dust. Black pestilence, the worst human battle.

PROPHECY OF PASSAU, GERMANY

(NINETEENTH CENTURY)

383. The whole country [Scotland] will become so utterly desolated and depopulated that the crow of a cock shall not be heard, deer and other wild animals shall be exterminated by horrid black rain.

BRAHAN SEER (1665)

384. A powerful wind will rise in the North, carrying heavy fog and the densest dust, and it will fill their throats and eyes so that they will cease their butchery and be stricken with a great fear.

HILDEGARD VON BINGEN (C. 1141)

385. The heretics are dead, captives exiled; blood-soaked human bodies, water, and a reddened, icy rain covering the entire Earth.

NOSTRADAMUS (1557) *C8 Q77*

ALTERNATIVE WORLD WAR III: THE WAR AGAINST HUMAN STUPIDITY

World War III seems unavoidable. However, the stresses of population and ecological collapse that may bring on the Balkanization of the world could also unite the world to put to an end the fossilized traditions and historical bad habits that threaten the future of humanity. The military-industrial complex could become a humanitary-industrial complex.

386. The aimless army will depart from Europe and join up close to the submerged island. The Arton [anagram for "NATO"] fleet folds up its standard: the navel of the world substituted by a greater voice.

NOSTRADAMUS (1555) *C2 Q22*

387. These . . . ruinous wars shall pass away and the "Most Great Peace" shall come.

'ABDU'L-BAHA' (C. 1890) God Passes By

388. They shall beat their swords into plowshares, and their spears into pruning hooks: nation shall not lift up sword against nation, neither shall they learn war any more.

ISAIAH (738–687 b.c.) *Isa. 2:4*

389. The American federal government will reforest all waste areas and the headwaters of all major rivers. Anyone who cuts down a tree will be legally responsible for planting another one in its place. We will also have a national policy for flood and pest control and for irrigation.

DAVID GOODMAN CROLY (1888)
Glimpses of the Future

390. Prepare yourself for the final war of the future: The armies of the nations are moving into position. Jets are taxiing on airfields, ready to take off. Fifty million soldiers advance into the battle-field-and-stream, forests and mountains. The allied nations of the entire earth are poised to spend $1.5 million a minute and are prepared to suffer hardships at home to ensure victory for all.

But this war is not to be nuclear. It will not see civilization extinguished in thirty minutes. In fact, this war could go on for a few centuries.

We can call it World War *Green*: the war to end all wars. This war pits our armies, with their logistical powers and sophisticated "weaponry," against the causes of planetary destruction. The vast amounts of genius and wealth that have been stockpiled for bloodshed are finally being used for healing and enriching the earth.

391. Rather than starving our human enemies, we starve all potential for violence by using our resources to sustain the flow of food and clothing to the needier nations.

392. Rather than dig trenches, the armies scoop out furrows for the planting of wheat. Tanks become tractors. A Maginot Line of dams captures water in parched lands and fires its salvos of water into lines of irrigation ditches.

393. Soldiers search for land mines without explosives—a treasure trove of untapped wells—and helicopter gunships drop organic pesticides on the swelling Third World armies of locusts. Millions of villages are defended from ignorance with forts of education.

JOHN HOGUE (1990)
The Millennium Book of Prophecy

○ ○ ○ ○ ○ ○

IS THE WORLD REALLY GOING TO END?

○ ○ ○ ○ ○ ○

SIGNS IN THE SKY

When a biblical or pre-twentieth-century prophet declares that signs in the sky will herald the end of the world, many of us might take that to mean light shows made by little gray aliens in UFOs. Actually the signs already exist. The blinking lights of passenger jets run across the stars and moon and the brush strokes of vapor they leave across blue skies would adequately terrify any prophet living before the modern era of flight.

394. I will show wonders in the heavens.

JOEL (C. 600 B.C.) *Joel 2:30*

395. The world will be lit by a fiendish red light.

PROPHECY OF LA SALETTE (1846)

Perhaps with the term "red" she describes the orange-hued streetlights of today's cities?

396. Before a great cross in the sky, they lacerated their own faces and tore their hair. I saw flames of devastated cities, others completely covered by flood; only a few roofs, chimneys and tree tops were protruding. Still other cities were completely devoured by the earth, while the red of the sky persisted.

MARIA AND ELSA OF VOLTAGO, ITALY

(1937)

397. The Purification will begin shortly after humans build a great house in the sky [a space station?]. By then there will be fires everywhere and greedy, selfish, power-mad leaders, internal wars. This is the last danger sign.

HOPI PROPHECY (PRE-COLUMBIAN)

398. Samarobrin [enigmatic name for a space station?], one hundred leagues from the hemisphere [240 miles above the Earth]. They shall live without law, exempt from politics.

NOSTRADAMUS (1557) *C6 Q5*

399. And there shall be signs in the sun, and in the moon, and in the stars. . . . Mens' hearts failing them for fear, and for looking after those things which are coming on the earth: for the powers of heaven shall be shaken.

JESUS CHRIST (a.d. 30–33) *Luke 21:25–26*

400. Near the day of the Great Purification, there will be cobwebs spun back and forth in the sky.

HOPI PROPHECY (PRE-COLOMBIAN)

401. And the sun became black as sackcloth of hair, and the moon became as blood; and the stars of heaven fell unto the earth, even as a fig tree casteth her untimely figs, when she is shaken of a mighty wind. And the heaven departed as a scroll when it is rolled together; and every mountain and island were moved out of their places.

ST. JOHN OF PATMOS (a.d. 81–96)

Rev. 6:12–14

402. I saw also many cradles with children swing on the water. I understood it as a sign that only children will be saved from the general destruction.

MARIA AND ELSA OF VOLTAGO, ITALY

(1937)

Saviors of the World Coming Out of the Clouds

403. And while they looked stedfastly toward heaven as he went up, behold, two men stood by them in white apparel; which also said, Ye men of Galilee, why stand ye gazing up into heaven? this same Jesus, which is taken up from you into heaven, shall so come in like manner as ye have seen him go into heaven.

LUKE (FIRST CENTURY a.d.)

Acts 1:10–11

404. And then shall appear the sign of the Son of man in heaven . . . and they shall see the Son of man coming in the clouds of heaven with power and great glory.

JESUS CHRIST (a.d. 30–33)

Matt. 24:30

405. And then shall they see the Son of man coming in the clouds.

> JESUS CHRIST (a.d. 30–33)
>
> *Mark 13:26*

406. Vishnu will return as Kalki, the White Horse, as the last Avatara [Hindu Messiah] . . . will also descend on a White Horse in a tornado of fire.

> *Various Hindu Puranas (c. 3000 B.C.)*

407. And when these things begin to come to pass, then look up, and lift up your heads; for your redemption draweth nigh.

> JESUS CHRIST (a.d. 30–33)
>
> *Luke 21:27*

408. The Lord [Kalki] will appear in His divine form consisting of Sattva [purity] alone, for the protection of virtue.

> Srimad Bhagavata Purana *(before A.D. 300)*

409. The veil hath fallen away, the curtain is lifted, the clouds have parted, the Lord of Lords is in plain sight—yet all hath passed the sinners by.

> 'ABDU'L-BAHA' (C. 1920), PARAPHRASING MUHAMMAD Selections

Buddha's Advent as "Maitreya"

> *Buddha prophesied that he would return to earth again in twenty-five hundred years as a world teacher called "Maitreya" (meaning "The Friend").*

410. When the Buddha [in Spirit] hears the hour strike, he will send Maitreya Buddha—after whom the old world will be destroyed.

H. B. BLAVATSKY (1888)
The Secret Doctrine

Earth's Trial by Messianic Fire

411. The Lord . . . is a consuming fire.

MOSES (C. 1300 b.c.) *Deut. 4:24*

412. The Lord Jesus shall be revealed . . . with his mighty angels, in flaming fire.

ST. PAUL (C. a.d. 51) *2 Thess. 1:7–8*

413. And I saw heaven opened, and behold a white horse; and he that sat upon him. . . . His eyes were as a flame of fire . . . and he had a name written, that no man knew, but he himself. And he was clothed with a vesture dipped in blood: and his name is called The Word of God.

ST. JOHN OF PATMOS (a.d. 81–96)
Rev. 19:11–13

414. But the day of the Lord . . . the heavens shall pass away with a great noise, and the elements shall melt with fervent heat, the earth also and the works that are therein shall be burned up.

> ST. PETER (C. a.d. 64) *2 Pet. 3:10*

415. All spiritual discipline stands devoured by the wild fire of Kali Yuga [unconsciousness and sin of the final age].

> Srimad Bhagavata Purana *(before A.D.
> 300)*

416. Alternative "bloomsday" prophets collectively agree that if there is any divine fire coming to burn the earth, it is burning and purifying the love and awareness of people in a more enlightened age and that these prophecies above should not be taken as literal fire burning people.

> VARIOUS PROPHETS

FINAL WARNINGS BEFORE THE END OF THE WORLD

Many prophetic traditions give us final signs to punctuate the end of time.

The Hopi Final Warnings

417. Metal wires hung like ropes are suspended in the air [telephone and power lines].

418. The "Gourd of Ashes" will be thrown from the sky which will burn the land and boil the oceans [atomic bombs].

419. The apocalypse will begin when the white man builds a permanent house in the sky.

420. The white man will disturb the sacred mesas of the Hopi land searching for precious metals.

421. A man will bring back a piece of the moon.

422. If we dig precious minerals from the land we will all perish.

423. There will come a great multitude from the direction of the East who dress in red. This tribe of the "red cap, red cloak" will slowly disappear from sight. Their tracks become broken and finally vanish in a field shown on the sacred tablet.

> The red-cloaked followers of Osho (Rajneesh) visited America during the 1980s. They stopped wearing their distinctive red clothes and went underground (vanished). Currently America is visited by greater numbers of red-robed lamas associated with the Dalai Lama.

424. You will know the time of purification is near when the land of Turtle Island sees the coming of three great symbols: the Sun, the Swastika, and the great red color.

> Hopi elders believe these symbol-forces came during World War II in the guise of America's enemies: the "sun" (Imperial Japan), the Swastika (Nazi Germany) and the great red (Communism).

St. Xavier's Body Lies Molding in the Grave

425. In the sleepy Indian state of Goa stands the five-hundred-year-old Basilica of the Bom Jesus. One can escape the heat and glare of the tropical midday sun and find within the dark interior of a side chapel the cool-to-the-touch silver coffin of St. Francis Xavier. The citizens of this former Portuguese colony will tell you that the body has remained uncorrupted by the tropical climate for five centuries.

The mummified saint is a desiccated device of prophecy. It is foretold that when Xavier's corpse begins to rot, you can set your watch for the onslaught of the latter days. All local claims to the contrary, one need only regard the current state of the Jesuit cadaver-under-glass to confirm that the beginning of the end time has begun.

JOHN HOGUE (1990)
The Millennium Book of Prophecy

Three Final Warnings Before the End of England

St. Columbcille of Ireland, in A.D. 522, foresaw three final warnings before the collapse of England at Judgment Day:

426.

1. The burning of the Tower of the great kings.
2. The conflagration of the Dockyard of the Galls.
3. The burning of the Treasury where gold is deposited.

In World War II German bombers set the Tower of London on fire as well as the dockyards of the east end of the British capital. To date this leaves one final warning unfulfilled, a fire in the British treasury. Perhaps the "fire" is metaphorical and refers to an adverse financial impact of the new European currency, the Euro?

St. Collumbcille's Final Warning for Ireland

427. Great shall be [Ireland's] renown and her power.

Ireland at the end of the 1990s is enjoying a time of plenty and economic boom thanks to its dominant position as the center of telecommunications and computer technology in the European Union. When I was in Dublin in November of 1998, I was struck by the vitality of the people, their fine clothes, and the general affluence of a country enjoying an average GNP boost of 12 percent a year.

428. Young women will become unblushing. There will be no standard by which morals may be regulated, and marriages will be solemnized without witnesses.

429. More unjust and iniquitous shall be every succeeding race of man!

The Kali Yuga: The Dark Age of Iron and Chaos

The final age of the Hindu cycle is symbolized either by Kali, the god of sin, or by a fierce, black-skinned goddess of the same name, who wears only a bloodstained smile. This sword-touting, demoniac deity is worshiped in India as the all-compassionate murderess, the butcher of our illusions. The accumulation of thousands of years of karmic excess may climax with Mother Kali banging at our door with the bill at the end of her age.

430. During the Kali age, people indulge in . . . theft, falsehood, deceit, vanity, etc., and delusion, hypocrisy, and vanity overshadow the people. And Dharma [religious seeking] becomes very weak in the Kali age.

431. [In the dark age of Kali] people commit sin in mind, speech, and actions.

432. Quarrels, plague, fatal diseases, famines, drought, and calamities appear.

433. Testimonies and proofs have no certainty. There is no criterion left when the Kali age settles down. . . . People become poorer in vigor and luster. They are wicked, full of anger, sinful, false and avaricious. Bad ambitions, bad education, bad dealings, and bad earnings excite fear. The whole batch becomes greedy and untruthful.

434. Many *sudras* [untouchables] will become kings [today India has political leaders who are *sudras*], and many heretics will be seen. There will arise various sects; *sannyasins* [ascetics] wearing clothes colored red [Buddhists, Rajneeshees, Hare Krishnas, etc.]. . . . Many profess to have supreme knowledge, because thereby they will easily earn their livelihood.

435. In the Kali age . . . there will be many false religionists.

436. The country [India] will become desolated by repeated calamities, short lives, and various kinds of diseases. Everyone will be miserable.

437. Owing to the dominance of vice and Tamoguna [quality of darkness], people will freely commit the sin of abortion, on account of which there will be a decline in the longevity and strength of the people. The people will live up to 100 years at most.

438. In spite of all the Vedas [the Hindu Bible] being in existence, it would be as if there were no Vedas, and the performance of sacrifices would be stopped.

Matsya Purana *(A.D. 330)*

> Modern India mirrors the worst nightmares of Vedic seers of the righteous past: Abortion is rampant (so is overpopulation—a by-product of Vedic tradition); life expectancy in India is around forty-five years—one of the world's lowest averages; there is widespread illness and disease. Many Hindu priests bewail what they view as a loss of true religious sincerity, indicated first by the rise of Buddhism, and most recently by the gaggle of gurus like the Maharishi, or "the Bhagwan," who seduced Westerners and dressed them up as red-robed *sannyasin* pilgrims. However, not all lost "virtues" may be worth crying over. The breakdown of the inhuman caste system, which keeps a quarter of the Hindu population in slavery, or the decline of traditions like suttee (widows being burned alive on their husbands' funeral pyres) could be seen as a big improvement.

The Last Warning: A Plea to Stop Abusing the Earth—or Else

439. This planet is a living being. A high consciousness. The Earth is suffering. Waves of death spasms are passing through her body. Can't you hear her crying? Don't you see her situation? Can't you hear her shouting for help? She is beckoning her children to relent. But her children are turning their backs to her, and continue stumbling in the clouded labyrinth which they have created for themselves.

AMBRES (1986)

440. But it is the nature of life that it exerts its power to the last moment. Now the Earth has come to the last moment and is exerting its final effort. If those people who understand the situation the Earth is in would spread [that understanding] all over the world, the Earth would immediately start to exert its healing power and heal itself.

TAMO-SAN (1989)
Opening of the Treasure House

441. This need for a farsighted vision has been set aside for shortsighted egoistic thinking. The human being has to wake up from her sleep. She must look around herself to see what is happening. She must act. Before it is too late. Before the Mother [Earth] takes her children with her and disappears out of the flow of time.

AMBRES (1986)

442. Some parts of the Earth's healing process are often referred to by us as natural disasters such as earthquakes, floods, etc. We then try to interfere with the Earth's own healing process, rather than to cooperate with it. If we learn to cooperate with the power, the Earth itself will help us to clean up the unnecessary things that people have produced.

TAMO-SAN (1989)
Opening of the Treasure House

443. And the time is not far away, because the sleeping humanity has suffered much and is going to suffer more, and as the suffering grows deeper . . . it is a blessing in disguise. Man can tolerate only a certain quantity of suffering and then he wakes up. And man has suffered enough.

OSHO (1985) From Darkness to Light

444. We need to save what's left on this Earth, because the prophecies say that when the coyote and the crow and the Indian perish from this Earth, everybody, including all races, will die.

GRANDFATHER SEMU HUARTE (1983),
CHUMASH NATION

445. I am in favor of complete birth control for at least twenty years, so that the population of the world can be reduced to one-fourth. But the great servants of the people will not allow it to happen because if there are no poor people, no orphans, no starving nations, what will happen to these people like the pope, Mother Teresa, etc.? Just for their glory they need the world to remain in poverty.

OSHO (1985) The Last Testament

446. The people here now don't care about Mother Earth, because when they die, they're going to heaven. They're going to get a harp, a pair of wings, and a halo, and they're going to be playing all the time. It is very unattractive to me. I don't even know how to play a harp.

GRANDFATHER SEMU HUARTE (1983),
CHUMASH NATION

447. As far as the world of man is concerned, I don't think there is much chance of converting the masses against their own past. They are creations of the past, and their past will come to its crescendo in the coming crisis. The masses will be drowned in that crisis. I feel sad about it, but the truth has to be told.

OSHO (1988) Hari Om Tat Sat

448. The human's incredible fear of life and death is sharpening her judgments into weapons. She cuts the world into pieces, she creates territories, she builds walls and draws limits. She creates a false security for herself within her own family, the tribe, the group, the town, the country—although in reality there exists nothing separating one human being from the other or one group from the other, other than all the divine differences, the wonderful nuances and individualities.

AMBRES (1987) Ambres

449. Only a few people in the world will be able to survive after this global suicide, and those will be the people who are deeply rooted in consciousness: alert, aware, loving, and ready to disconnect themselves with the past completely and unconditionally, and ready to begin the New Man and the new humanity with the freshness of a child.

450. Their only hope is a self-realized being. It is too late to do anything to prevent the immense destruction that is going to happen. If we can protect only a few genuine human beings, that will be enough, more than enough. The past of humanity has been completely accidental; they have been doing things without knowing the consequences. Now we are suffering the consequences, and there is no way to change those consequences.

OSHO (1988) Hari Om Tat Sat

451. Many of the dreams or visions don't necessarily mean the end; they could also indicate a change. Our people say that people who are not spiritually in tune can't adapt to this change. They won't have the necessary physical, mental, and spiritual strength to change themselves. It is being said that humanity will become mad.

There will be an energy or something similar that will influence the atmosphere [radiation from ozone holes?]. As a consequence, the pressure in our brain will increase by 35 percent. But people who have become spiritually clear and accept these approaching energies of the cosmos will be able to adapt to them and use them positively for themselves. They will find protected areas where they will be secure from this "human cleansing process."

452. Seventy to eighty percent of humanity are not spiritually but materialistically oriented. That's why they won't be able to endure this transformation; they will go mad. They will kill themselves and destroy everything around them. It will be like a madhouse. Probably somebody will then push the famous button because of this.

TIM SIKYEA (1988), YELLOWKNIFE
TRIBE, CANADIAN DENEE INDIANS

453. Mankind will be decimated by epidemics, famines, and poison. After the catastrophe they will emerge from their caves and assemble, and only a few will have been left to build the new world. The future is approaching at a quick pace. The world will be destroyed in many quarters and will never be the same as before.

SEERESS REGINA (EARLY TWENTIETH
CENTURY)

454. Water and fire will purify the Earth, and the period of true peace will begin.

PROPHECY OF LA SALETTE (1846)

455. Times of disaster make you aware of the reality as it is. It is always fragile; everyone is always in danger. You just go on dreaming, imagining beautiful things for the coming days, for the future. But in moments when danger is imminent, suddenly you become aware that there may be no future, no tomorrow, that this is the only moment you have.

OSHO (1986) The Path of the Mystic

456. Through intense tribulation shall man be brought nearer to perfection and more fitted to enjoy the wonders of the new Aquarian Age, that, born in the blood and sacrifice, will in the end fulfill the meaning of its symbol "the Water Bearer," whose pouring out of water on the earth is the emblem of unselfishness—the negation of Self—arrived at through suffering.

CHEIRO (1926)
Cheiro's World Predictions

457. So times of disaster are very revealing. They don't bring anything new into the world; they simply make you aware of the world as it is—they wake you up. If you don't understand this, you can understand this, you can become awakened.

OSHO (1986)
The Path of the Mystic

DATING THE END OF THE WORLD

Some dates for the end of the world include:

458. 2000.

> VARIOUS PROPHETS OF ALL
> APOCALYPTIC RELIGIOUS
> DENOMINATIONS

459. 2001.

> PYRAMID AND CHRISTIAN PROPHECIES

460. September 2001.

> CHALDEAN PROPHETS (SECOND
> CENTURY b.c.)

461. 2012.

> THE MAYAN CALENDAR

The Mayan calendar, which only experiences a leap year once every 370,000 years, is the most accurate calendar of the ancients.

462. 3755.

In that year the sun suddenly expands into a red giant devouring the planets Mercury and Venus.

463. Later that year asteroids hit Earth. The resultant fire storms consume all life on the Earth's surface.

464. 3797.

Earth is consumed by expanding sun.

> NOSTRADAMUS (1555)
> *Preface to* Les Propheties

465. According to Nostradamus, after 3797, the sun ends its expansion with its new diameter extending a little farther than 93 million miles (the late great planet earth's orbit). Mars survives and the red planet continues its revolutions around the red sun.

466. The world will not end for at least another three thousand years.

ATTRIBUTED TO JEANE DIXON (C. 1970S)

467. For in those days shall be affliction, such as was not from the beginning of the creation which God created unto this time, neither shall be. And except that the Lord had shortened those days, no flesh should be saved: but for the elect's sake, whom he hath chosen, he hath shortened the days.

JESUS CHRIST (a.d. 30–33) *Mark 13:19–20*

468. When all the planets conjoin in the sign of Cancer and are so positioned that a straight line would pass directly through all their orbs, all things earthly will be consumed.

BEROSUS (SECOND CENTURY b.c.),
CHALDEAN PRIEST

469. According to Masoudi, a medieval Coptic historian, the Great Pyramid of Giza was built by King Surid to preserve the spiritual and mathematical knowledge of Egypt in a giant stone scripture that would weather not only the coming great flood, but a future world conflagration as well. Esoteric scholars claim that the Pyramid chronicles life from the time of Adam and Eve to the year 2001, when the world, as we are told by Surid's dream interpreters, will be destroyed by fire coming from the constellation of Leo.

470. Lord Buddha said that the Wheel of Dharma, which creates the momentum needed for a global search for truth, requires a new Buddha ("awakened one") to give it a fresh spin every twenty-five hundred years. He divides the cycle into five five-hundred-year intervals punctuated by a significant loss of momentum in the spiritual evolution of man. The first revolution starts around 500 B.C. with a push from Gautama Buddha; orbit number two pushes off the B.C. standard for a lunge into A.D. time with Christ; revolution three sees a weaker spin between 500 and 700, while China turned Buddhist and Islam was born; in 1000 Europe became Christianized and Asia turned Buddhist; an even more anemic turn of the Wheel around 1500 witnessed the birth of Sikhs and Protestants. The momentum of truth will grind to a halt by 2000.

JOHN HOGUE (1994)
The Millennium Book of Prophecy

471. Aquarius is only at the commencement of his reign. War, destruction, bloodshed, and famine are the instruments of his purpose . . . by which he destroys convention and enthrones "the new" on the ruins of the old.

CHEIRO (1925)
Cheiro's World Predictions

472. The Golden Age of Shambhala [the Mongolian-Tibetan version of the reign of the messiah on earth] ends after eighteen hundred years. Some prophecy watchers believe the world will end afterward. If the King of Shambhala comes out of hiding to save the world around the year 2000, then the Tibetan prediction for end of the world is set for the same time as Nostradamus's, between 3797 to 3800.

VARIOUS TIBETAN SEERS (C. 1000)

473. Yes, all the predictions of the ancient seers, like Nostradamus, that the world is going to end by the end of this century are true in a very different sense than it has been understood.

OSHO (1986)

DESCRIBING THE END OF THE WORLD FROM A COSMIC SOURCE

474. When nights will be filled with more intensive cold and days with heat, a new life will begin in nature. The heat means radiation from the earth, the cold the waning light of the sun. Only a few years more and you will become aware that sunlight has grown perceptibly weaker. When even your artificial light will cease to give service, the great event in the firmament will be near.

475. The nebula of the Great Bear will have arrived in the region of the earth and finally will fill the space of five hundred suns at the horizon. It will more and more cover up the light of the sun until the days will be like nights at full moon. The illumination will not come from the moon, but from Orion, which constellation, by the light of Jupiter, will send forth its rays on the Great Bear and will dissolve its nebula with the force of light.

476. By this time mankind and the animal kingdom will have been stricken with terror. Birds will be like reptiles and will not use their wings. Animals of the ground, in fear and alarm will raise such a clamor that it will make human hearts tremble. Men will flee into their homes in order not to see the macabre occurrence. Finally complete darkness will set in and last for three days and three nights.

477. During this time men, deprived of the power of light, will fall into a slumberlike sleep, from which many will not awaken, especially those who have had no spark of spiritual life. When the sun will again rise and emerge, earth will be covered by a blanket of ashes like snow in winter, except that the ashes will have the color of sulfur. Damp fog will ascend from the ground, illuminated by igneous gases. Of Mankind there will be more dead than there had been casualties in the world wars. . . . On the seventh day after the return of light earth will have absorbed the ashes and formed such a fertility as has not been experienced ever before.

478. But Orion will cast down its rays on earth and show a path toward the last resting place of the greatest and most eminent man who had ever lived on earth. The survivors will proclaim his ancient doctrine in peace and will institute the millennium, announced by the Messiah, in the light of true brotherly and sisterly love, for the glory of the Creator and for the blessedness of all mankind.

JOHANN FRIEDE (D. 1257)

479. A very mighty quake in the month of May. Saturn in Capricorn. Jupiter and Mercury in Taurus. Venus also in Cancer, Mars in Virgo: [At that time] hail will fall greater than an egg.

NOSTRADAMUS (1557) C10 Q67

This rare astrological configuration will take place forty-two years before Nostradamus's predicted end of the world, A.D. 3797. When the sun expands into a red giant, the Earth will experience tremendous gravitational and climatic stresses.

JUDGMENT DAY PROPHECIES

480. But those who live the century through
In fear and trembling this shall do,
Flee to mountains and the dens,
To bog and forest and wild fens—
For storms shall rage and oceans roar
When Gabriel stands on sea and shore;
And as he blows his wondrous horn,
Old worlds shall die and new be born.

MOTHER SHIPTON (C. 1561)

481. For the day of the Lord is great and very terrible: and who can stand it?

JOEL (C. 600 B.C.) *Joel 2:11*

482. Brothers kill brothers, and even children spill one another's blood. Everyone steals and hoards great wealth, and sensual sin prevails. The end of the world is nigh—yet men are hard and cruel, and listen not to the doom that is coming. . . . No one heeds the cries of his neighbor, or lifts a hand to save.

The Ragnarök

483. The sign that the judgment has begun will come in a cold winter night with the rumbling of thunder and the trembling of mountains. Fasten the windows and doors, cover all lookouts. Your eyes should not see the most terrible of all happenings, because God's wrath is holy. He will purify the earth for you, the small number of the faithful. Convene in prayers before my crucifix and invoke the guardians of your soul.

Medieval manuscript, author unknown
(c. 1257)

484. And the kings of the earth, and the great men, and the rich men, and the chief captains, and the mighty men, and every bondsman, and every free man, hid themselves in the dens and in the rocks of the mountains; and said to the mountains and rocks, Fall on us, and hide us from the face of him that sitteth on the throne, and from the wrath of the Lamb: for the great day of his wrath is come; and who shall be able to stand?

ST. JOHN OF PATMOS (a.d. 81–96)
Rev. 6:15–17

485. When the priests and princes who follow Falsehood come to Thy Judgment Bridge, for all time they shall dwell in the abode of Untruth [Hell].

ZARATHUSTRA (c. 1700 b.c.)
Zend-Avesta *Ys. 46:11*

486. When the Son of man shall . . . sit upon the throne of his glory. And . . . he shall separate them one from another, as a shepherd divideth his sheep from the goats. And he shall set the sheep on his right hand, but the goats on his left. Then shall the King say unto them on his right hand, Come, ye blessed of my Father, inherit the kingdom prepared for you from the foundation of the world. . . . Then shall he say also unto them on the left hand, Depart from me, ye cursed, into everlasting fire. . . . And these shall go away into everlasting punishment: but the righteous into life eternal.

JESUS CHRIST (a.d. 30–33)
Matt. 25:31–34, 41, 46

487. Allah the Exalted will return some of the dead people to the present world in the same physical bodies they had before. Allah will do this to honor one group and to condemn another, to grant superiority to the faithful over the disbelievers, and to judge between the oppressors and the oppressed.

AL-MUFID (D. 1022) Awa'il al-Maqalat

488. And it shall come to pass in that day, that I will seek to destroy all the nations that come against Jerusalem.

ZECHARIAH (C. 160 b.c.) *Zech. 12:9*

489. And I saw an angel come down from heaven, having the key of the bottomless pit and a great chain in his hand.

ST. JOHN OF PATMOS (a.d. 81–96)
Rev. 20:1

490. And at that time shall [archangel] Michael stand up, the great prince which standeth for the children of thy people: and there shall be a time of trouble, such as never was since there was a nation even to that same time: and at that time thy people [the Jews] shall be delivered, every one that shall be found written in the book [of life]. And many of them that sleep in the dust of the earth shall awake, some to everlasting life, and some to shame and everlasting contempt.

DANIEL

(SIXTH–FOURTH CENTURY b.c.)

Dan. 12:1–2

491. For unless mankind uses these years to smooth out past karma and prepare for the spirit state, the opportunities may not come again for thousands of years, inasmuch as the human population will be decimated and opportunities for entering physical bodies will be slim.

SPIRIT GUIDES OF RUTH MONTGOMERY

(1979) *Strangers Among Us*

492. At the end of Kali-yuga . . . the Lord will appear as the supreme chastiser.

Srimad Bhagavata Purana

(before A.D. 300), 2.7.38

493. And he shall judge among many people, and rebuke strong nations afar off.

MICAH (C. 721 b.c.) *Mic. 4:3*

494. [After the apocalypse] Then will shine forth the effulgence of divine mercy, supreme justice having punished all evildoers.

ST. CAESARIUS OF ARLES (a.d. 470–542)

495. By his irresistible might he will destroy . . . all whose minds are devoted to iniquity.

Vishnu Purana *(c. A.D. 300–1000)*

The Second Judgment

496. And when the thousand years are expired, Satan shall be loosed out of his prison, and shall go out to deceive the nations which are in the four quarters of the earth, Gog and Magog, to gather them together to battle: the number of whom is as the sand of the sea. . . . And fire came down from God out of heaven and devoured them. And the devil that deceived them was cast into the lake of fire and brimstone . . . and shall be tormented . . . forever and ever. And I saw a great white throne, and him that sat on it, from whose face the earth and the heaven fled away; and there was found no place for them. And I saw the dead, small and great, stand before God; and the book was opened, which is the book of life: and the dead were judged out of those things which were written in the books, according to their works. And the sea gave up the dead which were in it; and the death and hell delivered up the dead which were in them: and they were judged every man according to their works. And death and hell were cast into the lake of fire. This is the second death. And whosoever was not found written in the book of life was cast into the lake of fire.

St. John of Patmos (a.d. 81–96)
Rev. 20:7–15

497. God possesses the key to everything. Blessed who will then be still able to praise him [after the apocalypse], having obeyed all his commandments.

PASTOR BARTHOLOMAEUS
HOLZHAUSER (C. 1642)

498. Finally, it will be understood that the end of the world was merely a kind of purification.

MARIO DE SABATO (1971)

DOOMSDAY BODY COUNT

499. Only one-third of humanity will survive crossing the great mountain pass of time.

DEGUCHI NAO (C. 1896)
Omotto-Shin'Yu

500. If only one-third of humanity will survive it is better!

MEISHU-SAMA (1955)

501. A third part of mankind [was] killed by the fire and by the smoke, and by the brimstone.

ST. JOHN OF PATMOS (a.d. 81–96)
Rev. 9:18

502. The blind leadeth the blind into a ditch.

JESUS CHRIST (a.d. 30–33) *Matt. 15:14*

WHOSE RELIGION WILL RULE THE NEW HEAVEN AND EARTH?

In both the Judeo-Christian and Shambhala-Tibetan messianic traditions, a preliminary Judgment Day sees the Western messiah or Eastern avatar rule an enlightened theocratic world government for a thousand years. After this, in the Western messianic tradition, a second and final judgment will take place, dividing the souls of humanity between the forever forgiven and the forever condemned.

503. Only the Jews are the "Chosen People" and only their faith will survive the holocaust. Jerusalem will be the religious capital of the world.

VARIOUS JEWISH PROPHETS

504. The Twelfth Imam, or Mahdi, i.e., Messiah, will come and see all other faiths put to the sword. Only Islam will survive. Jerusalem will be returned to the faithful, and Mecca will be the capital of the Earth.

VARIOUS ISLAMIC PROPHETS

505. A new Buddhist Messiah called Maitreya ["the friend"] will incarnate and bring all the world's people back to the Dharma—the path of [Buddhist] truth.

VARIOUS BUDDHIST PROPHETS

506. Only Sikhs will survive the holocaust. I guess Jerusalem will move to Amritsar, Punjab.

VARIOUS SIKH PROPHETS

507. Nonaboriginal peoples can wake up before they destroy the planet; however, if they do not reconnect with the Earth they will perish, and only the native peoples will survive to build a new world.

VARIOUS NATIVE PROPHETS

WHAT IS NEEDED TO AVOID DOOMSDAY

508. I don't believe the human race will commit suicide, but it will stop just short of that.

ARNOLD TOYNBEE (1975)

509. I absolutely believe that no one wants to choose suicide. Up to now man has been surviving without transformation because there was no urgency for change.

OSHO (1984)

510. The sole means now for saving of the beings of the Planet Earth would be . . . that every one of these unfortunates during the process of existence should constantly sense and be cognizant of the inevitability of his own death, as well as the death of everyone upon whom his eyes or attention rests. Only such a sensation and such a cognizance can now destroy the egoism completely crystallized in them that has swallowed up the whole of their Essence.

G. I. GURDJIEFF (1924–27)
Beelzebub's Tales to His Grandson

511. I say unto you there is no evil, and there are no evil forces in the world. There are only people of awareness and there are people who are fast asleep—and sleep has no force. The whole energy is in the hands of the awakened people. And one awakened person can awaken the whole world. One lighted candle can make millions of candles lighted without losing light.

OSHO (1986)

512. There is no time to waste in any unconscious consolations. An immediate transformation is absolutely needed; it is an urgency which man has never faced before. In a way you are unfortunate that soon there will be no future. In another way, you are very fortunate because this crisis is so big—perhaps it may help you to wake up.

OSHO (1987) The Hidden Splendor

513. In order to know the future it is necessary first to know the present in all its details, as well as to know the past. Today is what it is because yesterday was what it was. And if today is like yesterday, tomorrow will be like today. If you want tomorrow to be different, you must make today different.

G. I. GURDJIEFF (1915)
Quoted in P. D. Ouspensky,
In Search of the Miraculous

514. Don't think about the world, think about yourself. You are the world, and if you begin to be different the world begins to be different. A part of it, an intrinsic part, has begun to be different: the world has begun to change.

OSHO (1987) The Greatest Challenge

515. We are always concerned with changing the world. That is just an escape. I have always felt that people who are concerned with others changing are really escaping from their own frustrations, their own conflicts, their own anxieties, their own anguish. They are focusing their minds on something else, because they cannot change themselves. It is easier to try to change the world than to change oneself.

OSHO (1987) The Greatest Challenge

516. To speak the truth they will have closed mouths.

NOSTRADAMUS (1555) *C5 Q96*

517. Only when there are many people who are pools of peace, silence, understanding, will war disappear.

OSHO (1979)

Zen: The Path of the Paradox

THE BOOK OF LAST CHANCES

Every limit placed on what we call the universe is eventually broken. We say humans will never break the sound barrier or live in space, and not long afterward the barrier is blasted and astronauts dance in zero gravity. We are also told that no one can soar beyond the barrier of accepted moralities. This, too, will be transcended in time—if there are enough future moments left for humankind to live.

The belief barrier stands to break us and all our tomorrows.

Here is a small selection of the prophetic pressure exerted down through the ages for us to drop old ideas and outmoded moral standpoints before they drop us into a catastrophe.

518. One may imagine the sight of billions of ants on board a driftwood, floating on a fast-running stream. The ants are apparently unaware that their driftwood is nearing a cataract. They seem to be even ignorant of the fact that they are on a driftwood. If they were aware, how could they afford to hate one another, scheme against one another, and be occupied with greed and hostility?

The moment when their driftwood falls down the cataract, what would anything mean to one or another ant, friend or foe?

This pathetic sight is nothing but an epitome of today's mankind.

TAMO-SAN (1957) Moor the Boat

519. If people would change their minds and really be spiritual, there would be no need for arms and fighting. Everything could be settled by speaking the truth. But now, people wouldn't know the truth if you spoke it. It only upsets them. It hurts their ego. And then you are their enemy.

GRANDFATHER SEMU HUARTE (1983),
CHUMASH NATION

520. According to the Sacred Hoop and the prophecies, it is time to share this ancient wisdom. . . . It is time for the Great Purification. We are at a point of no return. The two-legged are about to bring destruction to life on earth. It's happened before and it's about to happen again.

521. The earth People [indigenous natives] never wrote anything down, had no written language. They knew that if they wrote anything down it would be disastrous. If you write something down, you don't have to remember it. And mind goes off into unconsciousness. It becomes negative, or unconscious force.

Brave Buffalo (1985), Brule Sioux
Nation

522. The prime cause for all these happenings is racial, national, religious, and political prejudice, and the root of all this prejudice lies in outworn and deep-seated traditions, be they religious, racial, national, or political. So long as these traditions remain, the foundation of human edifice is insecure, and mankind itself is exposed to continuous peril.

'Abdu'l-Baha (1920)

523. The pacifist theories, the conventional ethical codes of the world, and the international goodwill movements are all but void in coping with the ultimate catastrophe that mankind as a whole is now facing. So are Communism, Democracy, and whatnot. The history of man has witnessed great statesmen, great thinkers, great inventors, and great scientists who have accomplished so many great works. And mankind has worked day and night so hard to disseminate education, to imbue people with numerous ideologies, thoughts, systems, and all the nice things.

To our regret, all these efforts have not proven rewarding. On the contrary, human conscience has kept on disrupting, social turmoils accelerating, and accidents and natural calamities adding their frequency and scale. This is owing to the grave illusion underlying man's life outlook itself. The error was so fatal at its source that the entailing outcomes have formed a huge stream of incongruities during a long passage of time. Thus it is obvious that any deliberations or efforts, so long as the human behaviors—economic, political, educational, etc.— remain to be derived from the keynote of that root illusion, will work against their intentions as they have done in the past.

TAMO-SAN (1957) Moor the Boat

524. We have done enough stupidities. We have done enough harm to nature, to ourselves. We have been a nuisance on the earth. Our whole history is a history of crimes—man against man, man against nature. What have we been doing here? Why should we be bothered to survive? . . . What have you done in the thousands of years that you have been here? Can you justify that your being here on the Earth has been a creative addition to existence? Has it made it more blissful, more peaceful, more loving? Has it changed nature for something better?

What have you done in thousands of years except killing, murdering, butchering, slaughtering? And in beautiful, good names: in the name of God, in the name of truth, in the name of religion. It seems you want to kill and destroy, and any excuse is enough.

Perhaps it is better that this world does not survive. But I am saying "perhaps"—remember that. Again perhaps. . . .

The whole humanity perhaps may not be able to survive, but the few, a chosen few, can be saved. And that's enough.

OSHO (1985)
From Misery to Enlightenment

525. It may be that the revolutions and upheavals we see around us on all sides may for the time being bring about the fall of Empires, the destruction of Thrones, the death of the "old" and the birth of the "new."

526. It may be that times of great tribulations lie in store for humanity—I am, however, such a believer in the ultimate perfection of divine Design that I see in the symbol of the Aquarian Age the promise of "the Water Bearer" pouring out water on the earth, that in the end seeds may have more richness, flowers more fullness, and all sections of humanity more love for one another.

CHEIRO (1926)
Cheiro's World Predictions

527. There are two systems of power: one creative and one destructive. If the human being is using only the destructive power, then it will become suicidal. For a start it can look as though it is creative, but very soon it will show itself to be destructive. And the more technology is involved in it, the stronger it will accelerate, so that at the end the creative power cannot balance the destructive.

528. The human being has to awaken the force of love in the long run, whereas the negative force is shortsighted and hard. It can live longer in its aggressivity and build stronger and stronger momentum so that it can even kill the power of love.

529. Sometimes the human being says god is evil, god creates war. How can god condone destructive weapons; how can god condone starvation? Cannot the human being see that she is the one who has created the wars out of her fear generated by negative force? Can she not see that she has created the starvation, that she has created the different cultures and traditions which allow starvation?

530. She has created the different religions which fight with each other and kill each other. In war human beings are standing against each other and shouting, "It is a holy war, god is with us." Do you think god is fighting with himself or that there are different gods? No, the human being is fighting because of her fear. She has pushed away her paradise and she closed her eyes to paradise. And she doesn't see that she is really right in the middle of it.

AMBRES (1985)

531. Look at the world. Though people have been trying to do even a hundred good deeds, the world has been getting worse and worse. But why? It is because that which people have been trying to do is minor goodness, and they have forgotten the existence of major goodness.

532. The Earth has come to the verge of destruction. Its survival depends on our actions at this very moment. But dear friends, we are in the Dark Age and it is impossible to make right actions in the darkness. Thus it is of vital importance to bring Wisdom Light. When the Wisdom Light appears in the world, the darkness will disappear. And we will become able to see clearly and understand truly what is right to do and what is wrong to do. Then the Dark Age will transform into the New Age. When the nature of Wisdom Light is recognized in the world immediately, the New Age begins.

TAMO-SAN (1989)
Opening of the Treasure House

533. Behold, I will create new heavens and a new Earth. The former things will not be remembered, nor will they come to mind.

ISAIAH (FOURTH CENTURY b.c.) *Isa. 65:17*

○ ○ ○ ○ ○ ○

SATANS AND SAVIORS

○ ○ ○ ○ ○ ○

Before the true redeemer comes to save the world, his doppel-gänger from hell tries to deceive the world as its deliverer. Still, it all depends on your point of view. One religion's Christ is another religion's Antichrist.

ANTICHRIST LINEUP FOR THE TWENTY-FIRST CENTURY

General

534. Then shall they deliver you up to be afflicted and shall put you to death: and you shall be hated by all nations for my name's sake. And then many shall fall away, and shall betray one another; and shall hate one another. And many false prophets shall rise, and shall lead many astray. And because iniquity hath abounded, the charity of many shall grow cold.

JESUS CHRIST (a.d. 30–33) *Matt. 24:9–12*

535. [After 1970:] The forerunner of the Antichrist will assemble an army of men drawn from many nations, united under his banner [Islamic/Christian?]. He will lead them in a bloody war against those still faithful to the living God.

PROPHECY OF LA SALETTE (1846)

536. Shortly the kingdom of Christ will be founded on this Earth, but in the meantime, the prince of this world has been permitted to found a kingdom of his own, which will be only an empty mold of the undivided kingdom of Christ. Many members of the church will not see the difference, because even they seek the temporal, and they will be deceived by the prince of this world [the Antichrist].

EMELDA SCOCHY (1933)

537. One who the infernal Gods of Hannibal [Baal Hammon] will cause to be born, terror to all mankind. Never more horror nor the newspapers tell of worse in the past, then will come to the Italians through Babel [Iraq].

NOSTRADAMUS (1555) *C2 Q30*

Nostradamus foresaw three Antichrists. Two have already existed: Napoleon (*Napaulon*) and Hitler (*Hister*). A third Antichrist may come from the regions in North Africa and the Middle East where people once worshiped the Baal gods.

538. The enemies of peace, the dissolute ones, after having overcome Italy, the bloody black one of the night.

NOSTRADAMUS (1555) *C6 Q38*

This is the first of a number of predictions by Nostradamus implying that Italy will become a major target for a terrorist Antichrist from North Africa and the Middle East.

539. Throughout Asia Minor [Turkey—Kurdestan] there will be a great prohibiting of outlaws. Even in Turkey, Iran, and Iraq, blood will flow because of absolving a young dark man filled with evildoing.

NOSTRADAMUS (1555) C3 Q60

540. In the land with a climate opposite to Babylon [Iraq] there will be great shedding of blood. Heaven will appear unjust both on land and sea and in the air. Sects, famine, nations, plagues, confusion.

NOSTRADAMUS (1555) C1 Q55

541. The Religion named after the ocean will overcome against the sect of the son Adaluncatif: the obstinate, deplored sect will be afraid of the two wounded Aleph and Aleph [Alif].

NOSTRADAMUS (1555) C10 Q96

Nostradamus often hid his messages in word games called anagrams. "Adaluncatif" can make the name Cadafi Luna or, better, Muammar Qaddafi of the crescent religion of Islam. It must be remembered that, as a sixteenth-century prophet, Nostradamus had a bias against Islam as strong as the one American psychics had against Soviets during the Cold War. The Christianized Jewish prophet may color his vision to see the Antichrist as Islamic.

542. Sooner and later you will see great changes made, extreme horrors and vengeances. For as the moon [of Islam] is thus led by its angel, the heavens draw near to the Balance.

NOSTRADAMUS (1555) C1 Q56

Gabreel (Gabriel) is the avenging angel of the Christian and the Islamic apocalypses. Nostradamus often uses the scales of justice as a symbol for democracy. As already hinted at, the terror of the Middle Eastern Antichrist comes from the skies (the heavens). Therefore this could mean that nuclear "fires from the skies" will descend on the Western democratic powers sometime as early as 1999-2000. The quatrain indexing may target the year 1956, which saw the first successful victory of pan-Arab nationalism against the

West during the Suez Canal incident, when Egyptian president Gamal Abdel Nasser nationalized the Suez Canal and forced French and British forces to withdraw.

543. The Antichrist returns for the last time. . . . All the Christian and infidel nations will tremble . . . for the space of twenty-five years.

NOSTRADAMUS (1557)
Epistle to Henry II

Mabus: Nostradamus's Third Antichrist

544. Mabus will soon die, and then will come a horrible destruction of people and animals. At once one will see vengeances [from] one hundred powers, thirst, famine, when the comet [Hale-Bopp?] will pass.

NOSTRADAMUS (1555) *C2 Q62*

Mabus, a prime candidate for Nostradamus's third Antichrist, is the first to die in his war. The implication is that he is a terrorist whose dreadful act of destruction carries him off, but leaves reverberations and wars waged among a hundred nations for what Nostradamus says elsewhere in his prophecies could last twenty-seven years. Many Nostradamus watchers believe "Mabus" seen reversed in a mirror resembles the name "Saddam" (Saddam Hussein).

545. Between two rivers [Tigris and Euphrates] he will fear the military hand. The black and angry one will make him repent of it.

NOSTRADAMUS (1555) *C6 Q33*

546. He will enter, wicked, unpleasant, infamous, tyrannizing over Mesopotamia [Iraq]. All friends made by the adulterous Lady: the land dreaded and black in aspect.

NOSTRADAMUS (1557) C8 Q70

One's projections often get caught in the flypaper of Nostradamus's obscurity. This prophecy could adequately describe the ascent of Saddam Hussein and perhaps refers to the subsequent alliance of some Arab states with America in Operation Desert Storm.

Alus Sanguinaire: Nostradamus's Third Antichrist

547. His hand [or power] finally through the bloody Alus [Mabus?]. He will be unable to protect himself by sea.

NOSTRADAMUS (1555) C6 Q33

Many interpreters believe this implies the U.S. smart bombs that can strike Saddam Hussein's military assets launched from off shore. Lesser-known terrorists like Osama bin Laudin suffered from the same powerlessness when U.S. ships launched cruise missiles to strike his terrorist bases in Afghanistan in 1998.

548. Roman [Italian] power will be quite put down, following the footsteps of its great neighbor. Secret hatreds and civil disputes will delay the crassness of these buffoons.

NOSTRADAMUS (1555) C3 Q63

The original French adverb for putting someone "down," *abas*, matches the spelling of the enigmatic name "Mabus."

549. A burning torch will be seen in the night sky near the source of the Rhône.

Famine and war will come, and help will be too late, when Iran mobilizes to invade Macedonia.

NOSTRADAMUS (1555) C2 Q96

The Antichrist uses regional ballistic missiles to strike Italy and southern France.

The Beasts of the Prophet Daniel

550. Daniel spake and said, I saw in my vision by night, and, behold, the four winds of the heaven strove upon the great sea. And four great beasts came up from the sea, diverse one from another. The first was like a lion, and had eagle's wings: I beheld till the wings thereof were plucked, and it was lifted up from the earth, and made stand upon the feet as a man, and a man's heart was given it.

And behold another beast, a second, like to a bear [Russia], and it raised up itself on one side, and it had three ribs in the mouth of it between the teeth of it: and they said thus unto it, Arise, devour much flesh.

After this I beheld, and lo another, like a leopard, which had upon the back of it four wings of a fowl; the beast had also four heads; and dominion was given to it.

DANIEL

(SIXTH–FOURTH CENTURIES b.c.)

Dan. 7:2–6

Christian interpreters believe these animal metaphors represent the evolution of great empires leading to a future revitalized Roman Empire led by the Antichrist.

Daniel's Ten-horned Beast

551. After this I saw in the night visions, and behold a fourth beast, dreadful and terrible, and strong exceedingly; and it had great iron teeth: it devoured and brake in pieces, and stamped the residue with the feet of it: and it was diverse from all the beasts that were before it; and it had ten horns.

I considered the horns, and, behold, there came up among them another little horn, before whom there were three of the first horns plucked up by the roots: and, behold, in this horn were eyes like the eyes of man, and a mouth speaking great things.

I beheld till the thrones were cast down, and the Ancient of days did sit, whose garment was white as snow, and the hair of this head like the pure wool: his throne was like fiery flame, and his wheels as burning fire.

A fiery stream issued and came forth from before him: thousand thousands ministered unto him, and ten thousand times ten thousand stood before him: the judgment was set, and the books were opened.

I beheld then because of the voice of the great words which the horn spake: I beheld even till the beast was slain, and his body destroyed, and given to the burning flame.

As concerning the rest of the beasts, they had their dominion taken away: yet their lives were prolonged for a season and time.

> DANIEL
> (SIXTH–FOURTH CENTURIES b.c.)
> *Dan.* 7:7–12

Millennium fever among Christian apocalyptic interpreters has caused them to currently divine the ten horns to each stand for a European leader or nation in the New Rome of the European Union—a supernation that has brought unity and peace to most of Europe and that many Christian fundamentalists view as a threat to the world.

The Beast of Revelation

552. And I stood upon the sand of the sea, and saw a beast rise up out of the sea, having seven heads and ten horns, and upon his horns ten crowns, and upon his heads the name of blasphemy.

And the beast which I saw was like unto a leopard, and his feet were as the feet of a bear, and his mouth as the mouth of a lion: and the dragon gave him his power, and his seat, and great authority.

And I saw one of his heads as it were wounded to death; and his deadly wound was healed: and all the world wondered after the beast.

And they worshipped the dragon which gave power unto the beast; and they worshipped the beast, saying, Who is like unto the beast? who is able to make war with him.

And there was given unto him a mouth speaking great things and blasphemies; and power was given unto him to continue forty and two months.

And he opened his mouth in blasphemy against God, to blaspheme his name, and his tabernacle, and them that dwell in heaven.

And it was given unto him to make war with the saints, and to overcome them: and power was given him over all kindreds, and tongues, and nations.

And all that dwell upon the earth shall worship him, whose names are not written in the book of life of the Lamb slain from the foundation of the world.

ST. JOHN OF PATMOS (a.d. 81–96)
Rev. 13:1–8

One might say either that it is easy to see how St. John stole his vision from an earlier prophet or that, because this vision is several centuries closer to the events, it is clearer in the details. Evangelical Christians use this passage to describe the Antichrist, who suffers a head wound that later is miraculously healed. He then becomes the ruler of the new Europe. He makes a pact with a false Jewish prophet masquerading as the returned Jewish messiah in Israel.

The Lord of "Childish Intellect"

553. The Tibetan prophecies of Shambhala, like the Western Antichrist traditions, also see an all-conquering man of evil, known as the Barbarous King of Childish Intellect. The King of Shambhala will come out of his mythic and secret kingdom and defeat this Eastern Antichrist in a battle similar to that of the Christian and Jewish Armageddon.

VARIOUS TIBETAN AND MONGOLIAN
SEERS (C. 1000)

The American Antichrist

554. The one who will pretend to be the Christ [has] already been born in [America]. . . . He presently resides in a Maryland suburb of Washington, D.C. A schoolboy now, he is handsome, gregarious, and well liked by his friends. His parents are attractive, well-bred people, and his father is a lawyer.

SPIRIT GUIDES OF RUTH MONTGOMERY
(1979) Strangers Among Us

His Code Name Is "RAYPOZ"

555. Leave, leave Geneva [the United Nations] everyone! The grim reaper [Saturn] will change gold to iron [wealth to weapons]. Those against RAYPOZ [Israel, the EC, the UNO and USA] will be exterminated. Before the invasion the heavens will show signs.

NOSTRADAMUS (1557) *C9 Q44*

RAYPOZ could be a code name for the Antichrist according to some inter-preters of Nostradamus. It may be an anagram for the atomic weapons reac-tor at Osirak, the place where Saddam Hussein first tried to create an atomic bomb. Israeli jets bombed the facility in the early 1980s.

Pope Antichrist

556. The end of time is not far off, and the Antichrist will not delay his coming. We shall not see him and not even the nuns will follow him, but those who will come later will fall under his domination. When he comes, nothing will be changed, in the nunnery everyone will be dressed as usual; the religious exercises and the services will go on as usual . . . when the sisters will realize that the Antichrist is in charge.

BERTINE BOUQUILLON (1850)

557. And the Great Vicar in the cap [the pope] will be returned to his original state. But desolated, and then abandoned by all, he will turn to find the Holy of Holies [Rome] destroyed by Paganism, and the Old and New Testaments thrown away and burned. After that the Antichrist will be the infernal prince.

NOSTRADAMUS (1557)
Epistle to Henry II

MESSIAH LINEUP FOR THE TWENTY-FIRST CENTURY

Taken together, there are dozens of religions around the world whose members are convinced their savior—and only their savior—is coming to save the world sometime in the first fifty years of the twenty-first century. (I have written a more comprehensive examination of their appearances in the book Messiahs *[Element, 1999].)*

558. In the year 2400, a new Messiah emerges.

CHEIRO (1931)

Cheiro's World Predictions

559. Jesus Christ: His second coming is widely expected among all Christian and New Age sects sometime after the year 2000.

560. Osiris: The pyramid prophecies see the reincarnation of the Egyptian god taking place between 1953 and 2001.

561. Muntazar: The Islamic Messiah of the Sunni Muslim sect, he is the successor to Muhammad, who at the "end of time" will unite the races of the world through understanding.

562. The Sioux Messiah: A man in a red cloak coming from the East will restore the law of the Native American to North America.

563. The Indonesian Messiah: The twelfth-century Indonesian prophet Djojobojo foresaw the coming of a great "Spiritual King" from the West. He returns after the Dutch and Japanese occupations, and what sounds like an economic and social crisis after the severe end of the rule of the Indonesian dictator Suharto.

564. Pahána, the Hopi Messiah: The "true white brother" from the East will wear a red cap and cloak and bring two helpers holding the sacred symbols: the swastika, the cross, and the power symbol of the Sun (atom?). He will restore the native Indian version of righteousness.

565. Quetzalcoatl: The Aztec/Mayan Messiah will be an olive-skinned man with a white beard coming from the East to North America in an air canoe with many followers in red.

566. Amida Buddha: The Mahayana Buddhist Messiah, a great Christlike Bodhisattva, is scheduled to come twenty-five centuries after Lord Buddha (after the year 2000).

567. The Japanese Messiah: Several sects of Japanese Buddhism and Shintoism foresee a variant of the Buddhist Maitreya appearing after 8 August 1988 (8/8/88).

568. The Maori Messiah: Over a dozen Maori chieftains in New Zealand from the nineteenth through the early twentieth century have laid claim to the title.

569. The White Burkhan: The Messiah of Central Asian nomads, he will come when the people of the steppes have abandoned their ancient gods (Communist Russia was atheist). He will come to offer them and the entire human race a spiritual rebirth.

570. Immanuel, "The" Messiah: This is *the* Jewish Messiah, Emmanuel, the true messenger of Yahweh, the God of the Jews, who will restore them to their status as the Chosen People. Know his time has come when the State of Israel is restored and the holy temple in Jerusalem is rebuilt a third time. The cornerstone for the new temple was set in 1997.

571. Kalki the Avatar: The Hindu Messiah, also known as Javada, is the tenth and last avatar of the Hindu *yuga* (epochal) cycle. His final incarnation will appear from the West. Hindu scriptures depict him riding a white horse.

572. The Sinful Messiah: Appearing in the final days is a messianic figure who, unlike Christ, is not without sin. There's some parallel to the Elias and Enoch prophecies of Christlike figures who preach before the world domination of the Antichrist. David Koresh of the Waco cult believed he was this Messiah.

573. The Twelfth Imam: The Shiite Messiah has never died, but will reappear beside Jesus prior to Judgment Day to complete the Holy Qur'an.

574. The Nazi Messiah: A few days before he committed suicide, Adolf Hitler correctly foretold the Cold War and added that a new Fascist savior who would finish his work would arise again sometime in the 2020s.

575. Khidr: The Sufi Messiah is the mysterious guide of the Islamic spiritual underground. He is the Sufis' version of the Shiite Twelfth Imam and Muntazar of the Sunnis.

576. The Return of Krishna: Various Hindu prophecies state that when the world is in darkness, Krishna will reincarnate again. The ancient Hindu *Puranas* and the *Srimad Bhagavatam* state that we are living in the darkest times now. It is called the Kali Yuga, the age of iron and chaos.

577. Balder, Son of Light: The Vikings foresaw his coming after their version of the final battle of Armageddon, called Ragnarök.

578. Saoshyant: The Zoroastrian Messiah, like Zarathustra, is scheduled to come at the onset of the Zoroastrian twelfth millennium (A.D. 2000).

579. The Eskimo Messiah: The prophets of the Arctic foresee him to be an olive-skinned man with long beard and white hair who comes from the East.

580. Maitreya The Buddha: Maitreya, whose name means either "The World Unifier" or simply "The Friend," is the mainstream Buddhist Messiah. He is very human God-Man whom Buddha predicted will be his second coming and a greater awakened one than himself.

581. The Iroquois Messiah: A savior of the tribes of modern-day New York, New England, and Eastern Canada will come from the Eastern horizon in glory.

582. The Great Plains Messiah: A man in a red cloak, coming from the East, will restore the law of the Native American to North America. In 1872, the Sioux medicine man Black Elk declared that the white man's persecution of the Sioux would end when a messenger "painted bright red" would come from the eastern horizon.

583. The Ghost Dancers' Messiah: In the late nineteenth century the Paiute Indian prophet Wowoka He (1858–1932) conjured up and revised the Pale Prophet legend. He saw a vision of earthly paradise, with the game and buffaloes rising from the dead to crowd the plains once again. He saw the red and white peoples living as brothers who would restore Nature's balance. They would establish a golden age by purifying themselves of negativity through participation in a sacred dance that would link the living with the departed souls of all those lost in the Native American apocalypse.

584. Rudra Cakrin, the King of Shambhala: The Tibetans call him Rudra Cakrin or Rigden-jyepo. He is the king of the mystical realm of Shambhala. He is lord over a kingdom of unbelievable spiritual and temporal riches. When the world sounds the depths of its iniquity, the King of Shambhala will come forth from that dimension with his spiritual warriors from every land and wage the Asian version of Armageddon against an Asian-style Antichrist.

585. The Aeon: Aleister Crowley, the controversial English occult mystic and self-professed messenger of the Aeon, foresaw him as the Angel of the Last Judgment. The Aeon's chief element is the fire of purification. A reincarnation of the Egyptian god Horus, the Aeon appears after the old universe and the present-day civilization are destroyed.

586. Gessar Khan: The Shang Tang nomads of the frozen high desert at the roof of the world call their savior Gessar Khan.

587. The Arghati King, the Ruler of the World: Upon the high and frozen Shang Tang plateau in Tibet, the leather-skinned nomads of Mongolian origin weave tales of a legendary kingdom deep within the earth called Arghati. Deep in the womb of the earth, a great ruler known as the King of the World awaits more enlightened times when he and his people can emerge from their great cavern cities and impart their wisdom to the survivors of a coming holocaust.

If the birds should fall silent in the Himalayan valleys and if the herds of horses should stand still and dumb, the nomads of Central Asia will tell you that King Arghati is making new prophecies.

588. The Pale Prophet: From native nations of North and South America come a number of parallel legends of a great white teacher (or teachers) who disembarked from boats on the Pacific shores of pre-Columbian Peru around two thousand years ago. He was pale in complexion like a Caucasian. His hair was the color of ripe corn, and upon his chin was a short yellow beard. Other legends say he was one of a band of white mystics traveling through Central America and Mexico who caused a schism by teaching a gospel of peace and love. The Pale Prophet augured the coming Native American apocalypse before he left, after which he promised his return to redeem the lost spiritual soul of the Native American peoples.

589. The world awaits the Savior, but before his coming a great catastrophe is threatening. Fires burn at a distance, weapons rattle and bells sound alarm. We have to be vigilant and strong! . . . the earth will writhe in agony.

Seeress Regina (early twentieth century)

NOSTRADAMUS'S CLUES TO "THE MAN FROM THE EAST"

A number of Nostradamus's prophecies seem to chronicle today's new spiritual teachers and their movement. The pattern of these prophecies indicates the unique historical phenomenon we call the Human Potential or New Age movement.

Within this movement are many groups (both fraudulent and genuine) that experiment with alternative lifestyles, philosophies, and religions, often Eastern in origin, and practice new psychological and physical therapies. These groups, although not always in agreement over details, are mostly concerned with discovering new paths to world peace and ecological balance. All strive to awaken humankind to its potential for higher consciousness.

The prophet gives specific clues to the character of the coming new religion, its nondogmatic and individualistic teachings, and to the identification of its visionaries. (For a more comprehensive examination, please see my Nostradamus: The Complete Prophecies *[Element, 1997, reprinted 1999].)*

The clues and their corresponding quatrains are:

590. He will appear in Asia [and be] at home in Europe.

C10 Q75

591. The man from the East will come out of his seat, passing across the Apennines to see France. He will fly through the sky.

C2 Q29

592. He will fly through the sky, the rains and the snows and strike everyone with his rod.

C2 Q29

593. He will appear in Asia, at home in Europe. One who is issued from great Hermes.

C10 Q75

Hermes' religion was nondualistic; therefore we are looking at an Eastern religious teacher who is Tantric in his dogma.

594. A man will be charged with destroying the temples and religions altered by fantasy. He will harm the rocks [of dogma] rather than the living [believers]. Ears filled with ornate speeches.

C1 Q96

The man will be an eloquent religious revolutionary.

595. Against the red [clothed?] ones religions will unite.

C9 Q51

596. The rose [color] upon the middle of the world scene. . . . Then at the time of need the awaited one will come late.

C5 Q96

597. At the eve of another desolation when the perverted church is atop her most high and sublime dignity . . . there will proceed one born from a branch long barren, who will deliver the people of the world from a meek and voluntary slavery and place them under the protection of Mars. . . . The flame of a sect shall spread the world over.

Epistle to Henry II

The man from the East will have followers in a new religion that uses flame and the color red metaphors. They may even wear red clothes, as do Hindu, Buddhist, and Jain sects from the East.

598. Second to the last of the prophet's name, will take Diana's day [the moon's day] as his day of silent rest.

C2 Q28

599. The great amount of silver of Diana [moon] and Mercury [Hermes]. The images will be seen in the lake [the mind of meditation]. The sculptor looking for new clay. He and his followers will be soaked in gold [a Hermetic reference to the attainment of enlightenment].

C9 Q12

600. The Moon in the middle of the night. . . The young sage alone with his mind has seen it. His disciples invite him to become immortal. . . . His body in the fire.

C4 Q31

601. [He] will take Diana's day as his day of silent rest. He will travel far and wide in his drive to infuriate, delivering a great people from subjection.

C2 Q28

Gautama the Buddha (560?–483? B.C.) proclaimed that the "Wheel of Dharma"—the dynamo for human spiritual evolution—would be turned once every twenty-five centuries by a world teacher to generate human-kind's rise to new states of consciousness. A new turn comes at the end of this millennium. One of Nostradamus's main clues about the man who will initiate this "turn" of the "wheel" concerns deciphering his name. Apparently the world teacher's second, or middle, name means "moon." An additional clue comes in the form of the symbol of birds flying in the sky.

602. The soft voice of the sacred friend [i.e., Maitreya, "the Friend"] is heard under holy ground. The human flame shines for the divine voice. It will cause the earth to be stained with the blood of the celibate monks, and to destroy the sacred [or false] temples of the impure ones.

C4 Q24

The "friend" referred to in this quatrain destroys the organized religions with words of truth through the "human flame" of a new religion. In the original French the word "sacred" is represented by the word "saint" written in the archaic form with an "f" written for "s," thereby implying that the "saint" is "faint" or false.

603. Libra will see the western lands [America] to govern, holding the rule over the skies and the earth. No one will see the forces of Asia destroyed. Until seven [thousand years] hold the hierarchy in succession.

C4 Q50

The seventh millennium calculated by Nostradamus ends with the Judeo-Christian calendar year of 2000.

604. The year the great seventh number is accomplished, appearing at the time of the games of slaughter, not far from the age of the great millennium [2000] when the dead will come out of their graves.

C10 Q74

605. [During the war of the Antichrist] wars and battles will be more grievous than ever. Towns, cities, citadels, and all other structures will be destroyed. . . . So many evils by Satan's prince will be committed that almost the entire world will find itself undone and desolated. Before these events [the twenty-five-year war of the Antichrist] many rare birds will cry in the air, "Now! Now!" and sometime later will vanish.

(Epistle to Henry II)

An additional clue comes in the form of the new world teacher—or teachers—using the symbol of birds flying in the sky. This may also imply that they fly like "birds"—they are jet-setters.

THE COMING OF AN IMPERSONAL MESSIAH

606. The search for truth is neither new nor old. . . . Nobody is a founder in it, nobody is a leader in it. It is such a vast phenomenon that many enlightened people have appeared, helped, and disappeared.

OSHO (1986) Socrates Poisoned Again

607. The Uniter is going to be born here and it is going to come in plenty. It is not going to be only one human being, but many. And when the Uniter is born, it is going to grow and more and more humans are going to be included in the thoughts of the Uniter.

AMBRES (1985)

608. It is also true that the world is the Avatar. It is humanity as a whole that is the Avatar in human form, not some specific human individual. . . . Only the whole is the Divine Manifestation without exclusion. Therefore, the Guru is not the Avatar in that exclusive sense. Mankind is the Avatar.

AVATAR ADI DA SAMRAJ (1974)
The Garbage and the Goddess

609. As time goes by, human after human will contribute to the growth of the Uniter.

610. The Uniter is in opposition to the old thought and its ability to limit love. But the old thought was necessary for the new to be born [was the necessary manure for the flowering]. Everything is a oneness. All the new is not really new. All this has been spoken before by different masters of different times, but it is only now in this new time that it will be understood that it will be lived. Together all of you who are listening to this are the body of the Uniter, the body and the limbs. . . . Together you are the new thought of the new time.

AMBRES (1985)

THE BUDDHAFIELD

The authentic gurus of the paradoxical Aquarian Age will not be messiahs in the Piscean role of savior. They will simply be the way-showers for those who are rebellious enough to seek their own truth. The "messiah" of tomorrow is not a man, or even a son of man, but a spiritual force field generated by many human beings who share one thing in common—their individual search for themselves. Every seeker will be buoyed by the presence of the others' unique urge for spiritual transformation. Aloneness breeds togetherness. With their people, the Aquarian masters will dissolve themselves into a new phenomenon in the evolution of enlightenment, the mass presence of the greater Messiah called the Buddhafield.

611. Man has lived a long time the way he has lived [violently and unconsciously]. By the end of this century, a critical quantum leap is possible. Either man will die in a third world war or man will take a jump and will become a new man. Before that happens, a great Buddhafield is needed—a field where we can create the future.

> OSHO (1977) The Diamond Sutra

612. Tuning in to a fully developed Master Field, where all these evolutionary processes have already taken place, permits those changes to be magnified and quickened or, in effect, lived into that system without its having to pass through certain of the processes associated with the individual struggle to evolve.

> AVATAR ADI DA SAMRAJ (1978)
> The Enlightenment of the Whole Body

613. In the old days, evil things spread rapidly, but now good things spread rapidly. If you understand . . . everything begins to appear wonderful and beautiful, and it naturally makes people stop wasting or stop desiring unnecessary things. This awakening is contagious and it will be transmitted to everybody soon.

> TAMO-SAN (1989)
> Lecture for the Awakening of the
> Whole World

614. Only amateurs in the field of spirituality can claim . . . that they are the center of the world, that they are the only begotten son of God, that they are the saviors of the whole world, that they are the messengers of God. . . . They don't even understand a simple law, that everyone has to save himself, everyone has to be a savior unto himself. That is the only possibility.

615. But it is more than enough to be a center to yourself. Then your peace becomes infectious; then your silence starts spreading around, catching other people's hearts. Then your love starts overflowing and reaching unknown strangers, and giving their heart a new dance, a new song. But this happens naturally; you are not the doer of it.

OSHO (1987) The Rebel

THE CRITICAL MASS OF ENLIGHTENMENT

The critical mass of enlightenment can be defined as the smallest number of awakened human beings whose collective influence can initiate a significant shift in global consciousness.

616. I want to do a certain thing in the world and I am going to do it with unwavering concentration. I am concerning myself with only one essential thing: to set man free. I desire to free him from all cages, from all fears, and not to found religions, new sects, nor to establish new theories and new philosophies. Then you will naturally ask me why I go the world over, continually speaking. I will tell you for what reason. . . . If there are only five people who will listen, who will live, who have their faces turned toward eternity, it will be sufficient.

J. KRISHNAMURTI (1929)

617. Only one-tenth of 1 percent of humanity is needed to usher in world peace.

MAHARISHI MAHESH YOGI (C. 1980S)

618. Even if only a hundred people remember themselves, the world can be saved.

G. I. GURDJIEFF (C. 1920S)

619. Even if two hundred people are aflame, enlightened, the whole world will become enlightened, because these two hundred torches can give fire to millions of people. Those people are also carrying torches, but without any fire. They have everything, just the fire is missing. And when fire passes from one torch to another, the first torch is not losing anything at all.

OSHO (1980)

620. If in a single day everyone would now lay aside all animosities, and put aside selfish motives, the world would be revolutionized by nightfall. Such is the power of souls acting together to effect favorable change! If man elected to do so, he could bring the twenty-first century's wonders to this pathetic century overnight, by deliberately altering his thinking. This will not occur in the present century, alas, but it will begin to occur in the next century [the 21st].

621. It is that manifestation [the shift of the Earth's axis, which Montgomery's guides say is physical and other prophets claim is spiritual] which will so shock humanity that man will devote himself to helping others as himself, and good thoughts will project to such an extent that it will seem like a new race of human beings. Actually, it is merely a demonstration of what right-thinking can do.

SPIRIT GUIDES OF RUTH MONTGOMERY
(1979) Strangers Among Us

622. If we make good use of advances of science and we manage to avoid the destructiveness of science, then my understanding is the twenty-first century can be the most religious century on this Earth. The twenty-first century will give birth to so many Buddhas, so many Siddhas, so many enlightened ones: more than the whole history of mankind has ever produced.

623. The situation will be very much like that in science today: Do you know the ratio of scientists who are alive on Earth now to the number of scientists who existed in the whole of man's past? You will be amazed: 90 percent of all scientists are alive today. And in the whole history of man—for 10,000 years—only 10 percent existed. And today 90 percent are alive!

624. What happened? An explosion of science has happened. Precisely like this, the moment for an explosion in religion is drawing near. Ninety percent of all Buddhas will be alive in the twenty-first century. And all the Buddhas and enlightened ones of the past will account for only 10 percent.

OSHO (1979) Hansa To Moti Chugai

THE FUTURE OF NATIONS

IN GENERAL

625. Calamities may happen; wars, plagues and pestilence may destroy; nations may rise and fall or new nations be born; but behind all, the mystery of Design weaves, on the tapestry of Time, the pattern of *Purpose*.

> CHEIRO (1931)
> Cheiro's World Predictions

626. The United States will become the United States of North America.

> JOHN HOGUE, INTERPRETING DAVID
> GOODMAN CROLY (1888)

627. Palestine will be a full-fledged state by 2000, and by 2008 it will absorb the Kingdom of Jordan.

> JOHN HOGUE (1999)

628. Palestine and Syria will come under disturbing influences and considerable bloodshed there and in Iraq will result.

629. [In India] the religious laws will become widened to meet the demands of the "new age."

630. [In the new age] even the "caste" system will slowly alter to allow India to awaken to the call of the Aquarian influence spreading over the entire world.

631. Things might improve if Scotland had her own government and managed her own affairs; but knowing the patient nature of the Scots, I think such an event will be a long time in coming.

> More than sixty years have passed since this prophecy was published and only now is Scotland seriously moving toward self-government and autonomy.

632. South Africa and Africa generally will not advance rapidly like the rest of the world. Some hundreds of years must yet pass before its real wealth will be discovered.

633. [Australia in the new millennium:] Large numbers of Japanese will endeavor to enter the country. The immigration question will become a delicate problem for the government, in which Japan, as a nation, will become involved.

634. Turkey will make rapid strides toward advancement, both politically and in social reforms, but some extraordinary religious changes may be expected.

CHEIRO (1931)
Cheiro's World Predictions

635. King and emperor will disappear [from Germany], and another will lash the whip. An iron crown is for thee, German people, and it will press and weight heavily upon thee for many years to come [the crimes of Hitler and the Nazis]. Only long after will arise a new crown, not of iron, nor gold or silver, but of rays of light. And a man is holding it, of supreme power, and then the German nation will be standing the test, not with weapons of iron or brass, but with deeds high and lofty.

SEERESS REGINA (EARLY TWENTIETH CENTURY)

636. [Egypt becomes an Islamic fundamentalist state:] Wreck for the fleet near the Adriatic waters [a NATO fleet defeated in a future Balkan War]. The earth trembles, lifted into the air, placed on the land [a vast earthquake]. Egypt quakes, Mahometan augmented [political earthquake—Egypt is seized by a fundamentalist Islamic leader]. The Herald [President Hoshni Mubarak] surrenders himself [and] is commissioned to cry out.

NOSTRADAMUS (1555) *C2 Q86*

637. Through fire and arms not far from the Black Sea, He will come from Persia to occupy Trabzond [Turkey]: [Alexandria, Egypt] to tremble . . .

NOSTRADAMUS (1555) *C5 Q27*

638. Iran becomes a nuclear power by 2005.

VARIOUS FUTURE WATCHERS

639. France will endure a future dictatorship.

640. Mexico will undergo revolutionary change like Russia and India. It will rebel against religious dogma and outside interference from other countries.

CHEIRO (1931)
Cheiro's World Predictions

RUSSIA: THE HOPE OF THE WORLD

Edgar Cayce, Cheiro, and Nostradamus envisioned a future that might shock capitalists and Marxists alike. Russia will be the catalyst for world peace and brotherhood. The country has already achieved this in part by backing out of a four-decade standoff with the United States. Although Russia enters the new millennium in desperate straits, the next century apparently will see it resurrected as a spiritually enlightened nation—that is, if it doesn't drag the world down into a third world war.

641. The day will come when Russian waste of blood—the blood it has and will yet pour out like water—will make "a new heaven and a new Earth."

642. The mysterious Aquarian Age has commenced its dawn across the world, and already its first rays have revolutionized Russia.

CHEIRO (1926)
Cheiro's World Predictions

643. The communal law will be made in opposition. The old orders will hold strong, then [are] removed from the scene. Then [the old order of] Communism put far behind.

NOSTRADAMUS (1555) *C4 Q32*

644. [In Russia] a new understanding has come and will come to a troubled people . . . when there is freedom of speech, the right to worship according to the dictates of the conscience—until these come about, still turmoils will be within.

EDGAR CAYCE (1938) *No. 3976–19*

645. Russia, however, having for its zodiacal ruler the sign of Aquarius . . . and Uranus, will recover more quickly from revolutions or disaster and will advance more rapidly toward the achievement of its purpose than will Mexico or India.

CHEIRO (1931)
Cheiro's World Prediction

646. On Russia's religious development will come the greater hope of the world. Then that one or group that is the closer in its relationship [with Russia, i.e., the United States or possibly the European Union] may fare the better in gradual changes and final settlement of conditions as to the rule of the world.

EDGAR CAYCE (1932) *No. 3976–10*

647. I predict that Gorbachev is going to succeed in bringing the second and greater revolution to Russia; and his revolution in the Soviet Union is going to affect everything in the whole world.

OSHO (1987) The Rebel

648. A new idea of government will little by little spread from [Russia], which will completely revolutionize Europe, Asia, [and] the Far East; and Russia will become the most powerful nation in the history of modern civilization.

CHEIRO (1926)

Cheiro's World Predictions

649. What then of nations? In Russia there comes the hope of the world, not as that sometimes termed of the Communistic, or Bolshevik, no; but freedom, freedom! That each man will live for his fellow man! The principle has been born. It will take years for it to be crystallized, but out of Russia comes again the hope of the world.

Cayce closes his famous declaration about Russia's destiny by offering a challenge and a dose of compassionate criticism to Americans:

650. In the application of these principles, in those forms and manners in which the nations of the Earth have and do measure to those in their activities, yea, to be sure, America may boast; but rather is that principle being forgotten when such is the case, and that is the sin of America.

EDGAR CAYCE (1944) *No. 3976–29*

Apparently to Cayce, if Russia is tomorrow's great hope, America will nurture her transformation. An economic marriage between U.S. technology and Russian natural resources was foreseen by Edgar Cayce in 1932 during the Great Depression. The prophet cautioned a businessman:

651. Many conditions should be considered, were this to be answered correctly. You could say yea and no, and both be right, with the present attitude of both peoples as a nation, and both be wrong, for there *is* to come, there *will* come, an entire change in the attitude of both nations as powers in the financial and economical world. As for those raw resources, Russia surpasses all other nations. As for abilities for development of same, those in the United States are the farthest ahead. Then these *united* or upon an equitable basis would become or *could* become—powers; but there are many interferences. [These] . . . will take years to settle.

EDGAR CAYCE (1932) *No. 3976–10*

652. Remember what now I say, begin in Russia, finish in Russia.

G. I. GURDJIEFF (1949)

> The twentieth-century mystic made this prediction to his disciples a few weeks before his death. Russia was where he launched his spiritual movement for the "conscious evolution" of humankind. This admonishment points to the future completion of his great work through a renaissance of his primarily Eastern teachings in the former Soviet Union.

653. Russia seems to be a land of destiny, not only for its own people, but for the whole world. It was the first to revolt against capitalism; it is going to be again the first to revolt—against dictatorial communism. The future is of a democratic communism, a communism rooted in the freedom of man.

654. If [Gorbachev] can open the doors for a spiritual search, then certainly he can fulfill the prophecy of Edgar Cayce that Russia is the hope for all mankind.

OSHO (1987) The Golden Future

CHINA: THE NEXT SUPERPOWER

China will become a superpower in the early twenty-first century. Its rise to superpower stature will, however, depend largely on how other nations help or hinder its great destiny. China will become either the spokesman or the armory for the nonaligned nations of the Third World.

655. China? There lies a sleeping giant. Let him sleep! For when he wakes he will move the world.

NAPOLEON BONAPARTE (D. 1821)

656. Japan and China will unite politically and control Asia.

CHEIRO (1931)
Cheiro's World Predictions

657. The Antichrist, who was born in the Middle East in 1962, will galvanize the world with his charisma and false, though seductive, religious teachings. A strong U.S. ally, he will drag the last superpower and its western allies into a third world war with China by the 2030s.

ATTRIBUTED TO JEANE DIXON (C. 1970S)

658. Neither of the two adversaries will conquer or be vanquished. Both mighty ones [China and America?] will lie on the ground, and a new mankind will come into existence.

PASTOR BARTHOLOMAEUS
HOLZHAUSER (C. 1642)

659. Europe will suffer invasion by Asian hordes in the year 2009.

C. BILLENSTEIN (1920), A DANISH
ENGINEER AND PSYCHIC

660. Communist China will wage war with Russia and its satellite allies [implying the former states of the Soviet Union]. The war will last for seventeen years starting in 2020 [and going] through 2037.

ATTRIBUTED TO JEANE DIXON (C. 1970S)

661. What is the sin of China? Yea, there lives the quietude that will not be turned aside, saving itself by the slow growth. There has been a growth, a stream through the land in ages which asks to be left alone to be just satisfied with that within itself.

EDGAR CAYCE (1944) *No. 3976–29*

662. China will one day be the cradle of Christianity, as applied in the lives of men. It is far off, as man counts time, but only a day in the heart of God, for tomorrow China will awake.

EDGAR CAYCE (D. 1945)

663. In the early twenty-first century America will exert pressure on rival nations by using food exports as a political weapon against China. China in turn will forge political alliances with the oil-rich Central Asian countries and use oil and fossil fuels for leverage against America.

JOHN HOGUE (1988)

664. *Will there be war between China and the United States?*
A war will come, before which all previous wars will fade. Streams of fire will come from clouds, where are no clouds. And in the middle will be the great water [the Pacific?]. . . . Great armies with iron horses and dragons will be seen, and everything will be different than it has ever been. Battles will rage on and within the earth and in the air, and whole cities on this side and across the great water will be destroyed.

MARIENTHAL PROPHECY (1749)

665. The white men will battle against other peoples in other lands—with those who possessed the first light of wisdom. Terrible will be the result.

WHITE FEATHER (1958), HOPI BEAR
CLAN *Recorded by Rev. David Young*

The first known civilizations appeared in Mesopotamia (present-day Iraq), the Indus River Valley (the tense border region of modern Pakistan and India), and China. The People's Republic of China is set to rival America as a superpower in the early twenty-first century.

○ ○ ○ ○ ○ ○

THE FUTURE OF AMERICA

○ ○ ○ ○ ○ ○

THE DECLINE AND FALL OF THE AMERICAN SUPERPOWER

The millennium may be for the United States what the turn of the nineteenth to the twentieth century was for the British Empire— on the surface the empire appeared more powerful than any other nation on earth. Within fifty years it withered and disappeared. America's decline from superpower to simple nation may take less time.

666. New states will be carved out of Texas and California.

667. The population surrounding New York bay—including the Jersey shore—may decide to form a separate state.

DAVID GOODMAN CROLY (1888)
Glimpses of the Future

668. The American president will acquire greater and greater power.

669. The Senate and the House of Representatives will correspondingly lose power, being demoted to the status of yes-men.

670. The government will become increasingly corrupt and resort to dubious methods to maintain control.

671. Semimilitary organizations at the capital (like the Roman praetorian guard) will increase in power such that eventually they will control the presidency.

672. Eastern culture will heavily influence American thought in the years to come. Eastern cults and religions will gain strength here and finally supplant traditional Christianity. A new religion will combine Eastern and Christian concepts.

673. Americans will become less concerned with individual freedom and more concerned with security. Guaranteed incomes and ever more lavish television spectaculars will correspond to "bread and circuses."

674. America's technology will rise to new heights.

675. Armies will shrink in size. Americans will no longer be drafted (already a virtual certainty). Foreign nationals will be employed in peacekeeping operations.

676. America will become more and more dependent on importing goods for other countries.

677. The percentage of affluent Americans will continue to grow, as will their decadent excesses. Yet an influential minority will continue to fight to maintain older standards.

678. A clash with the "barbarians" (probably Russians) will weaken America, but put it into alliance with Russia. In fact, the clash may already have happened, being dubbed the Cold War, the Korean Police Action, and Vietnam. The alliance with the Soviet Union [Russia] should follow soon, but with America in a weaker position than now.

679. A Pax Americana—a period of relative lack of war— should be soon upon us. Optimism should run high, decadence should run wild, and the stage will be set for America to begin a search for new spiritual values.

ALAN VAUGHAN (1973)
Patterns in Prophecy

680. The process of destruction of this community America will proceed in consequence of organic abnormalities. In other words, the "death" of the first community came, as they say, from the "mind," whereas the death of the second community will come from the "stomach and sex" of its beings.

G. I. GURDJIEFF (1924–27)
Beelzebub's Tales to His Grandson

AMERICA'S NEXT CIVIL WAR

681. A body of censors will be created who will be responsible for policing the U.S. legislature at all levels.

682. Because our constitution is so inflexible, we will not be able to reform it. Instead, under the pressure of radical changes and perhaps a social war, we will adopt a new constitution.

DAVID GOODMAN CROLY (1888)
Glimpses of the Future

683. There will be great stress, as brother rises against brother, as group or sect or race rises against race—yet the leveling must come.

And only those who have set their ideal in Him and practiced it in their dealings with their fellowman may expect to survive the wrath of the Lord.

EDGAR CAYCE (1938)

684. Nation will rise against nation, kingdom against kingdom, states against states, in our own country and in foreign lands.

BRIGHAM YOUNG (D. 1877)

685. By the year 2026, the constitution of the United States will be redrafted. The American system of democracy will be unrecognizable compared to what it was in the 1990s. But this will not be a negative change. Chicago psychic Irene Hughes predicts that man will live in greater trust and love of his fellow man at that time.

JOHN HOGUE, INTERPRETING IRENE
HUGHES (1974)

686. There will be an erosion and breakdown of the American Dream, says Edgar Cayce, when those who lead it proclaim their might and power as being right, when the leaders of this land have brought "many of the isles of the sea and many of the lands" under their influence. A second civil war will come at a time when America as the supreme superpower fears no man or devil. At that time Cayce warns, "in their own land [Americans] will see the blood flow as in those periods when brother fought against brother" (No. 2976–24).

687. In 1939, Cayce gave his future countrymen an alternative to civil war when he warned that if all Americans of every class and color didn't seek a "universal oneness of purpose," America would suffer a second revolution (No. 3976–25). Lytle Robinson and other Cayce scholars interpret these events as the struggle of black brothers against white during the 1960s.

688. In the 1870s, Orson Pratt, one of the early fathers of Mormonism, described the coming Balkanization of America as a war pitting "neighborhood against neighborhood, city against city, town against town, state against state, and they will go forth destroying, and being destroyed. Manufacturing will almost cease, great cities will be left desolate.

JOHN HOGUE, INTERPRETING CAYCE
AND PRATT (1994)

AMERICA: THE FUTURE CRADLE OF NEW RELIGIONS

689. America, though it is spiritually childish, brash, and still capable of playing with nuclear fire, is fresh enough to take on a new religious dimension. There are some tentative signs that the first Eastern seeds have already sprouted in the American field of dreams. For over two centuries, the world has exiled its misfits and rebels to America. And within this melting pot of incongruous races, minds, and hearts has been a steady stream of experimental religious sects: the Quakers, Hutterites, Puritans, Mormons, and Shakers came from the fringes of Christianity in the last century; the Hare Krishnas, the Rajneeshees, the Moonies, and the Transcendental Meditators arrived in the present century. One of America's greatest attributes is its ability to give social and religious experiments a chance.

690. Before America can become the seat of a new religious world vision, it will have to experience the shattering of its dreams. America, as the Sioux medicine man Good Horse Nation says, must wake up. To do that, Americans will have to suffer a most difficult weaning—from what is false or destructive in the American Dream. The potential for social derailment is evident in the runaway pattern of crime, drugs, and violence of today's America. In the end, the coming social upheaval may be necessary to shock America back to consciousness before the Dharma can move to the "land of the red man."

JOHN HOGUE (1994)
The Millennium Book of Prophecy

○ ○ ○ ○ ○ ○

POLITICS

○ ○ ○ ○ ○ ○

THE END OF NATIONALISM

In the coming fifty years nationalism will go the way of the dinosaurs. The next great step in political history will be globalism.

691. Soon you will encounter a new world, fresh conceptions of the world, new organizations, new laws.

MADAME SYLVIA (1931)

692. There has arisen, and there is arising in the affairs and experiences of man everywhere, the necessity of there being not only so much consideration of a land as of all lands as a unit. For mankind is his brother, and thou art thy brother's keeper.

EDGAR CAYCE (1936) *No. 3976–16*

693. Two colossal nations will collapse, and as a result the political structure of governments will be transformed all over the world.

MADAME SYLVIA (1931)

694. Europe will become a unity of one nation, not many nations anymore. There will be different people and different souls, but not nations. I see one banner—white. In the middle of Europe—a tower. The map of Europe white, not bloody anymore.

MADAME SYLVIA (1948)

695. The United States will absorb Canada, Mexico, Central America, and the West Indies.

DAVID GOODMAN CROLY (1888)
Glimpses of the Future

696. The destiny of the world will be decided by a man with a pen and a man with a sword.

MADAME SYLVIA (1931)

697. America relinquishes its role as a superpower and becomes a member state of the Terran global nation by 2050. At that time international laws and a global constitution will be a higher law than its own constitution.

VARIOUS PROPHETS

698. Rather than a horrible conclusion to U.S. freedom, as feared by many survivalists and nationalists in 2000, America's national sacrifice will be viewed as its last great and visionary gesture as an independent nation. What started with America establishing a home for the United Nations, and generously sacrificing its bounty to rebuild Europe after the Second World War, will lead to its voluntary submission to a higher global government by 2050.

VARIOUS PROPHETS

699. Know that right, justice, mercy, patience . . . is the basis upon which the new world order *must* eventually be established before there is peace. Then, innately, mentally and manifestly in self prepare self for cooperative measures in all phases of human relations.

EDGAR CAYCE *No. 416–17*

700. Europe will become one united nation. There will be different people, unique souls, but not nations.

701. A new England will be created.

MADAME SYLVIA (1931)

702. In the time of those kings, the God of heaven will set up a kingdom that will never be destroyed, nor will it be left to another people. It will crush all those kingdoms and bring them to an end, but it will itself endure forever.

DANIEL

(SIXTH–FOURTH CENTURIES b.c.)

Dan. 2:44

703. The "religion of the heavens" is still the only religion by which God "talks with man" today as He did in the days of old. In the light of such knowledge, all mysteries will be made plain, God's message written across the heavens will in the end become correctly interpreted.

The language of stars, planets, and suns will translate "the Book" into words "understandable by the people." Nations will so realize their zodiacal affinities that they will group themselves together, and the unnatural frontiers of the present day will be swept away. Under such conditions war will become impossible and the "promise of peace" will at last be fulfilled.

> CHEIRO (1931), COMMENTING ON ISAIAH
> Cheiro's World Predictions

704. For I dipt into the future, far as human eye could see,
Saw the vision of the world, and all the wonder that would
be;

Saw the heavens fill with commerce, argosies of magic sails,
Pilots of the purple twilight, dropping down with costly
bales;

Heard the heavens fill with shouting, and there rain'd a
ghastly dew,
From the nation's airy navies grappling in the central blue;

Far long the world-wide whisper of the south-wind rushing
warm,
With the standards of the peoples plunging thro' the
thunderstorm;

Till the war-drum throbb'd no longer, and the battle flags
were furl'd

In the Parliament of man, the Federation of the world.

There the common sense of most shall hold a fretful realm in
    awe,
And the kindly earth shall slumber, lapt in universal law.

ALFRED, LORD TENNYSON (1842)
Locksley Hall, *ll. 120–130*

GLOBAL GOVERNMENT

705. With the present conditions then that exist—these have all come to that place in the development of the human family where there must be a reckoning, a point upon which all may agree, that out of all this turmoil that has arisen from the social life, racial differences, the outlook upon the relationships of man to the Creative forces or his God and his relationships one with another, must come to some COMMON basis upon which all MAY agree.

EDGAR CAYCE (1932) *No. 3976–8*

706. A new universal language will be created, which by a magic stroke will make everyone understand the other languages of Earth. It will be like a bridge, after the sudden perception that in all languages of the world lies a root of affinity on magical elements.

MADAME SYLVIA (1931)

707. [In the early twenty-first century:] And as if by instinct all will wish to have the same kind of representative government, so that each area will choose delegates to a world body that will oversee the Earth.

SPIRIT GUIDES OF RUTH MONTGOMERY
(1979) Strangers Among Us

708. The new era will liberate you from speech, because you will be able to sense what is in the thoughts of other men.

MADAME SYLVIA (1931)

709. By 2050 an entirely new United Nations will exist. It will be the United Parliament of Terra [Earth].

VARIOUS PROPHETS

710. Government will be of one type, with all sending delegations to occasional world parleys, and as the population increases [after the disastrous shift of the Earth's axis] there will be smaller units to handle local matters, but these will scarcely be needed because of the harmony among the people. National barriers will be nonexistent, as each strives for the good of all.

SPIRIT GUIDES OF RUTH MONTGOMERY
(1979) Strangers Among Us

711. Three hundred [nations] will be of one agreement and accord.

NOSTRADAMUS (1555) C5 Q37

712. By 2050, a sense of the individual's connection with the global collective will reach a new intensity borne by the pain and suffering of the previous two generations who endured the era of global and nationalistic collapse.

JOHN HOGUE (1994)

713. Thus it will be one government and one world, and the new currency to be introduced will be usable anywhere.

714. Color lines will be eradicated, because since the human soul is without color, skin tone has no meaning here.

SPIRIT GUIDES OF RUTH MONTGOMERY

(1979) Strangers Among Us

715. True civilization will unfurl its banner in the midmost heart of the world whenever a certain number of its distinguished and high-minded sovereigns—the shining exemplars of devotion and determination—shall, for the good and happiness of all mankind, arise, with firm resolve and clear vision, to establish the Cause of Universal Peace.

They must make the Cause of Peace the object of general consultation, and seek by every means in their power to establish a Union of nations of the world. They must conclude a binding treaty and establish a covenant, the provisions of which shall be sound, inviolable, and definite.

They must proclaim it to all the world and obtain for it the sanction of all the human race. This supreme and noble undertaking—the real source of peace and well-being of all the world—should be regarded as sacred by all that dwell on earth. All the forces of humanity must be mobilized to ensure the stability and permanence of this Most Great Covenant.

716. In this all-embracing Pact the limits and frontiers of each and every nation should be clearly fixed, the principles underlying the relations of governments toward one another definitely laid down, and all the international agreements and obligations ascertained. In like manner, the size of the armaments of every government should be strictly limited, for if the preparations for war and military forces of any nation should be allowed to increase, they will arouse the suspicion of others. The fundamental principle underlying this solemn Pact should be so fixed that if any government later violates any one of its provisions, all the governments on earth should arise to reduce it to utter submission, nay the human race as a whole should resolve, with every power at its disposal, to destroy that government.

717. Should this greatest of all remedies be applied to the sick body of the world, it will assuredly recover from its ills and will remain eternally safe and secure.

'ABDU'L-BAHA' (1875)
The Secret of Divine Civilization

718. The day we have unquestionable proof of the existence of extraterrestrial civilizations on distant stars, we will know that it is time for the childhood of humanity to come to an end. Our divided civilization will suffer a blow to its three hundred definitions of God, its nationalistic divisions, and any other dogma we cherished. The reality of "others" out there will make it necessary for us to abolish all our divisions overnight and work as one Human nation.

JOHN HOGUE (1996)

719. Soon will the present-day order be rolled up, and a new one spread out in its stead.

BAHA''U'LLÁH (1863) Kitáb-i-Aqdas

BEYOND DEMOCRACY

Often the current predominant form of political discourse believes that it is the last word in civic evolution. Monarchists and communists believed this; so do many today who believe democracy is the highest form of government. If prophecy teaches us anything, it shows us that everything changes, everything ends. Democracy will be transformed into something else. It is only a question of when.

720. Either there will be an ultimate war—which means death to all and everything—or a total change of the whole structure in the human society. I am calling that change "Meritocracy."

OSHO (1987) The Greatest Challenge

721. The Age of Pisces, with its ruler Jupiter—the God of Domination—is coming to a close; the dawn of Aquarius, with its ruler Saturn—symbol of Human Justice—*has already commenced.*

CHEIRO (1931)
Cheiro's World Predictions

722. Democracy will govern the world for the twenty-first century, but will be eventually replaced by a new form of government based on merit rather than political cunning. The political mind-set will eventually be exorcised out of politics. Government leadership will be a service people are trained for. Voters as well as candidates will need to prove their merit and qualifications to vote.

VARIOUS PROPHETS

THE FUTURE OF THE BRITISH ROYAL FAMILY

723. The young heir to the British realm, which his dying father had recommended to him; when the latter is dead, London will dispute with him, and from the son, the realm is demanded back.

NOSTRADAMUS (1557) C10 Q40

In one interpretation of this prediction, a future row between pro-monarchists and pro-republicans in the British Parliament sometime around 2040 leads to Prince William's abdication of the throne and Britain's move to become a republic.

724. Charles will become king of England after his mother steps down from the throne in the year 2008.

JOHN HOGUE (1997)
Nostradamus: The Complete
Prophecies

725. The day that she will be hailed as Queen, the day after the benediction, the prayer: The reckoning is right and reasonable, once humble never was one so trustworthy.

NOSTRADAMUS (1557) *C10 Q19*

This could be a vision of how people will regard Elizabeth II's legacy after she has either passed on or abdicated.

PRESIDENTIAL PREDICTIONS

I've been making presidential predictions since 1968. So far my track record has been 100 percent accurate. With that in mind, I sincerely hope that some of my predictions below will turn out to be wrong, especially those that warn of dangers to the future leaders of the United States.

726. President Clinton will complete his final term, despite all attempts to unseat him.

(1993)

727. By 2050, historians and public alike will view President Clinton as one of the three most important presidents of the 20th century (the other two being Franklin Delano Roosevelt and Richard Nixon). People in the mid–twenty-first century will view Clinton's sexual scandals with less cultural intolerance. They will focus more on his initiatives in foreign and economic policy that paved the way for a new era in international unity in the coming fifty years.

(1992)

I am compelled to enter this, even though my own personal opinions often disagree with the prophetic findings of my experiments. Still, such seemingly outrageous declarations from my "oracle" have often proved correct.

728. Arizona Republican Senator John McCain has the best chance to defeat Democrat Al Gore in 2000. However, the Republican party will suffer defeat once again, because it may choose another George Bush and a Dole as its candidates—to be exact, George W. Bush and a woman vice-presidential candidate like Elizabeth Dole or Senator Kaye Bailey Hutchinson of Texas.

(1998)

729. The Republican party will be a casualty of millennial fever. The right-wing fundamentalists in that party will split it apart over religious extremist views.

730. The next president will die in office, most likely in his first term.

(1994)

731. The next president will not be assassinated. He will succumb to health problems, perhaps heart trouble, or he will die in some air accident.

(1994)

732. It pains me to say it, but I believe that the president will be Al Gore. Although he may suffer an untimely death while in office, I can say that he will be remembered as a visionary leader, compared by some to President Kennedy. Like Kennedy, he will launch a national race—not the Space Race, but a race to make America ecologically responsible before it is too late.

(1992)

733. President Gore will have a woman as his vice president.

(1992)

734. A woman will be president much sooner than anyone expects. She will not be elected, but will become president upon the death of the president elected in 2000.

(1994)

735. Hillary Clinton will be a president of the United States before 2010.

(1998)

○ ○ ○ ○ ○ ○

SCIENCE AND TECHNOLOGY

○ ○ ○ ○ ○ ○

INVENTIONS

736. Instruments may be made by which the largest ships, with only one man guiding them, will be carried with greater velocity than if they were full of sailors.

737. [There will come] machines which enable men to walk at the bottom of the seas.

New energy sources will make fossil fuels obsolete:

738. By a machine three fingers high and wide and of less size a man could free himself and his friends from all danger of prison and rise and descend.

Antigravity bridges will float over the waters:

739. Bridges will be made without piers or other supports.

ROGER BACON (1220–92)

740. Aerial cars . . . will move through the sky from country to country; and their beautiful influence will produce a universal brotherhood of acquaintance.

ANDREW JACKSON DAVIS (1856)
The Penetralia

Mystery meets objectivity, and a new partnership is formed between science and mysticism:

741. Materialistic science will receive a deathblow. . . . One by one, facts and processes in nature's workshops are permitted to find their way into the exact sciences, while mysterious help is given to rare individuals in unraveling its arcana.

MADAME BLAVATSKY (C. 1888)

742. People will live beneath domes which will provide temperature-controlled environments and filter harmful substances out of the air.

DAVID GOODMAN CROLY (1888)
Glimpses of the Future

743. Diseases and pestilences extinguished, the world becomes small. For a long time the lands will be inhabited in peace. People will travel safely by air [over] land seas and wave.

NOSTRADAMUS (1555) *C1 Q63*

The Age of Aquarius will be the Age of Science:

744. The future belongs to the scientist, not to the politician. . . . [The politicians] will fade away on their own accord. They have been exploiting scientists for their own purposes, and to [exploit] anybody is not an act of dignity.

OSHO (1987) The Greatest Challenge

745. By that time a new kind of communication will have been established, with travel by spaceships throughout the globe, and magnetic and solar energies replacing fossil fuels.

SPIRIT GUIDES OF RUTH MONTGOMERY

(1979) Strangers Among Us

746. Computer by light-wave delivery will make all silicon-based technologies obsolete by 2030.

JOHN HOGUE (1993)

747. Novels will be transformed into a new kind of entertainment. Instead of employing real actors, as in a play, voices and visual images will be projected onto a stage, creating an illusion of reality.

748. Techniques to reproduce the great masters will be perfected so that most people will be able to afford their own gallery of fine art.

749. Compounds will be discovered which will have all the virtues and none of the defects of opium. They will enable us to experience magnificent visions while we sleep.

750. Printing will be fashioned in the colors of nature—blues, greens, browns, etc. Permanent literature will be printed in the most easily perceived color combination—yellow ink on a dark blue background.

DAVID GOODMAN CROLY (1888)
Glimpses of the Future

Was the dark blue background of today's computers foreseen?

Humankind will create a material as well as spiritual heaven on earth.

751. These improvements and discoveries will refresh the soul give it leisure and prepare it for a natural voyage to post-mundane climes. A glorious period is before mankind. It will be a kind of material heaven—a preparation for the Spiritual Harmonium. Fall in love with the new dispensation. . . . Have intelligent confidence in the advancement of the material world.

ANDREW JACKSON DAVIS (1856)
The Penetralia

GENETIC ENGINEERING

Much that is called criminal behavior will be found to be genetic, not psychological.

752. Legal measures will be instituted to prevent the criminal, the insane, and the diseased from bearing children.

DAVID GOODMAN CROLY (1888)
Glimpses of the Future

Genetic engineering will lengthen life.

753. Never again will there be in it [New Jerusalem] an infant that lives but a few days, or an old man who does not live out his years; he who dies at a hundred will be thought a mere youth; he who fails to reach a hundred will be considered accursed.

ISAIAH (FOURTH CENTURY b.c.)
Isa. 65:20

Through genetics humankind will see the end of death.

754. And God shall wipe away all tears from their eyes; and there shall be no more death, neither sorrow, nor crying, neither shall there be any more pain: for the former things are passed away.

ST. JOHN OF PATMOS (a.d. 81–96)
Rev. 21:4

AGING ENDS

755. Geneticists will unlock the secret of cell regeneration by 2030. They will perform the first successful experimental regression of aging by the 2090s. A man or woman of eighty will see his or her cells regenerated. An elderly person can become physically as young as an eighteen year old in the time of an average seven-year cycle of cell regeneration.

756. The end of aging will bring new benefits and problems. The complex moral issues about death and euthanasia will be turned upside down when people no longer die from old age, but will have to choose their death consciously. Is conscious death suicide or the climactic final gesture of a fully lived life?

JOHN HOGUE (1994)

○ ○ ○ ○ ○ ○

SOCIAL CHANGE

○ ○ ○ ○ ○ ○

*Historians say that the twentieth century saw as much social
change as the preceding nineteen hundred years. I would assume
it is possible, given the exponential transformations overtaking
society in the 1990s, that for better or worse the twenty-first century may see as much change as nineteen twentieth centuries.*

SOCIAL SCIENCE IN GENERAL

757. People will work no more than six hours at a time, and
this will be in staggered shifts. A whole range of goods and
services will be available during the nighttime hours.

DAVID GOODMAN CROLY (1888)
Glimpses of the Future

758. Virtual reality will cause a reality crisis in fifty years' time. When VR technologies can exactly mimic the world around us, the question will arise in many, "What's real?" In a hundred years' time technology will mimic virtual thoughts and emotions. In that far-off day the question collectively asked by humanity will be "Am I real?" A virtual reality crisis will bring new interest in spiritual awakening and foster a new science for understanding the consciousness of the soul—a mystery VR machines cannot artificially create.

JOHN HOGUE (1994)

759. Those who were in the realm for knowledge. . . . The learned and learning will not be of high value.

NOSTRADAMUS (1555) *C6 Q8*

760. A wave of social-political experiments will overtake civilization in the 2010s and 2020s. They will rival the experiments in communism, fascism, and democracy of a century earlier. Stresses in the world's social, economic sustainability will bring a return of the communist and fascist revolutions.

761. The breakdown of society in the 2020s could turn the world into a global Weimar Republic. Weimar was the seat of Germany's first fledgling democratic government established after the fall of the German monarchy after World War I. Political and economic stresses eventually overwhelmed the Weimar government and the Nazi dictatorship of Hitler took its place. Civilization across the world could be suffering the same stresses to sustain the needs and desires of two billion more consumers by the 2020s. Just as Germans in desperation turned to Hitler, the climate of frustration and hardship suffered by billions of disenfranchised young people will make them susceptible to the messianic promises of a hundred Hitlerlike saviors.

JOHN HOGUE (1997)

THE FUTURE OF THE RAT RACE

Will the Puritan work ethic—known by its critics as workaholism—derail in the new millennium?

762. By 2040 there will be one currency in the world, the Terra.

JOHN HOGUE (1999)

763. Scandinavian prophet Anton Johansson relates a scenario that could bankrupt a future American government through the violence of a single storm. He says that a hurricane will grow near Panama and then churn its way in a north-by-northeasterly direction, smashing into the American Gulf states and up the Mississippi Valley, gaining extra clout as it passed over the Great Lakes, rattling and rolling some of New York's skyscrapers to the earth. He says America will not be able to restore what was lost.

JOHN HOGUE, INTERPRETING ANTON
JOHANSSON (1989)

764. [In the Kali Age] Power will be the only factor determining righteousness and fairness. . . . Cunningness alone will be the motive force in business dealings. . . . Desire for riches will be the sole test of impiety and hypocrisy will be the only touchstone of goodness.

Srimad Bhagavata Purana
(*before* A.D. 300)

765. This know also, that in the last days perilous times shall come. For men shall be lovers of their own selves, covetous, boasters, proud, blasphemers, disobedient to parents, unthankful, unholy. Without natural affection, truce breakers, false accusers, incontinent, fierce, despisers of those that are good, traitors, heady, high-minded, lovers of pleasures more than lovers of God: Having a form of godliness, but denying the power thereof: from such turn away.

ST. PAUL (C. a.d. 40–50) 2 *Tim. 3:1–5*

766. This is a revelation of events of a universal character, which must shortly come to pass. Their spiritual outlines are now before my eyes. I see floating upon the sea of human fate the huge silhouette of a nude woman. She is—with her beauty, her poise, her smile, her jewels—a super-Venus. Nations rush madly after her, each of them eager to attract her especially. But she, like an eternal courtesan, flirts with all. In her hair—an ornament of diamonds and rubies—is engraved her name: "Commercialism." As alluring and bewitching as she seems, much destruction and agony follow in her wake. Her breath reeking of sordid transactions, her voice of metallic character, like gold, and her look of greed, are so much poison to the nations who fall victims to her charms.

LEO TOLSTOY (D. 1910)

767. Modern industry will tear away from the family the sentimental veil and reduce it to a mere money relation.

KARL MARX (D. 1883)

768. Man's answer to everything has been *power*—power of money, power of position, power of wealth, power of this, that, of the other. This has *never* been God's way, will never be *God's* way.

EDGAR CAYCE (1932) *No. 3976–8*

769. Wealth and piety will decrease day by day, until the world will be wholly depraved. Then property alone will confer rank; wealth will be the only source of devotion.

Vishnu Purana *(c. A.D. 900), 4:24*

770. And so the gods will depart from mankind—a grievous thing!—and only evil angels will remain, who will mingle with men, and drive the poor wretches by main force into all manner of reckless crime, into wars, and robberies, and frauds, and all things hostile to the nature of the soul.

771. Darkness will be preferred to light, and death will be thought more profitable than life. . . . The pious will be deemed insane, and the impious wise; the madman will be thought a brave man, and the wicked will be esteemed as good.

HERMES TRISMEGISTUS (a.d. 150–270)
Asclepius III

772. Of course, such a "record" will only lead to this, that the already sufficiently trifling size of their ill-fated planet will become, even in their bobtailed being-picturings of reality, completely trifling.

773. Whatever speed they may obtain with this "machine" of theirs [the car] all the same, if they remain as they are not only they themselves, but even their thought will never go any farther than their atmosphere.

G. I. GURDJIEFF (1924–27)
Beelzebub's Tales to His Grandson

774. In that day men will throw away to the rodents and bats their idols of silver and idols of gold which they made to worship.

775. Those who are not embroiled, mere spectators—good men as well as bad, wise men as well as fools, rich and poor, old and young—all are fish panting in the stream of poisoned waters.

TAMO-SAN (1960) Look Here!

776. Those countries which you now think of as closed will soon be open. And those countries you now think of as most open will soon be closed.

777. The inherited fear since millennia—suspicion from the beginning of time, combined with fear of losing possessions and properties—has created a greedy, intolerant, and directly suicidal human being. Progress is measured in coins and commodities, and those who have made collecting and owning their goal, in the richest and most materialistic countries, are guarding their possessions. Armies are patrolling boundaries and walls. Watchtowers and customs agents make sure the borders are not trespassed; passports and visas give some people permission to temporarily visit and travel in parts of the planet which belongs to you all.

Don't you see how ridiculous all this is? Don't you respond to the causes and laws which have created this life-negative way of living?

Start questioning what's happening around you, and go into your own depth and ask what you would like to change.

AMBRES (1987) Ambres

778. Raise not democracy nor any other name above the brotherhood of man, the Fatherhood of God!

EDGAR CAYCE (1939) No. 3976–24

779. You are ready now. You can trigger it [global suicide] . . . so that you don't waste the tremendous accumulations of your money and toil or don't betray the great producers of all these preparations, whom you have supported, admired, and thanked so much. You have elected to leadership of your governments and all other walks of life those people who you thought were most steadfast in making these preparations with persistent efficiency and boldness, to take advantage of any and all resources of entire nations. They are by no means to blame. They have been chosen by you to accomplish the showdown of your subconscious wills. They are therefore your godchildren.

TAMO-SAN (1957) Moor the Boat

780. These are signs of a decadent society, a society which has come to a suicidal point—a society which itself does not have any reason to live, and feels: Why should anybody else have any reason to live? The whole thing depends on America because America is in a hurry to go into a third world war. . . . The danger is from the White House in Washington. That is the most dangerous place on the Earth today. . . . There is still time for the people of America to prevent the catastrophe from happening. If the people of America cannot do anything, then these politicians are going to drag the whole of life on this Earth to the graveyard.

OSHO (1986) Transmission of the Lamp

Politicians have brought this great challenge to the whole of humanity. In a way we should be thankful to these fools.

OSHO (1987)

781. The global suicide is the ultimate outcome of all our cultures, all our philosophies, all our religions. They have all contributed to it in strange ways—because nobody ever thought of [the needs of] the whole.. . . . Hell is your fear projected. Heaven is your greed projected.

OSHO (1986)

782. It may be that the revolutions and upheavals we see around us on all sides may for the time being bring about the fall of Empires, the destruction of Thrones, the death of the "old" and the birth of the "new."

CHEIRO (1926)

Cheiro's World Predictions

783. Human society is not harmonious because each individual is divided inside, and his divisions are projected onto society.

OSHO (1989)

THE NEW WOMAN

Astrological prediction tells us that a "feminine" age like the closing two-thousand-year epoch of Pisces is expressed in patriarchal ways. Indeed the last two thousand years have seen a level of male domination over women in all forms of religion and society. The new Aquarian Age, being a "masculine" era, will be expressed in matriarchal ways. That may mean that either women will dominate or more than half the human race will finally gain equality.

784. Women throughout the world will enjoy increased opportunities and privileges. Along with this new freedom will come social tolerance of sexual conduct formerly condoned only in men. In addition, because of the greater availability of jobs, more women will choose not to have children.

DAVID GOODMAN CROLY (1888)
Glimpses of the Future

785. Even in such old civilizations as China and Japan, in spite of the most rock-bound laws of dynasties and religions, women have everywhere thrown off their shackles.

CHEIRO (1926)
Cheiro's World Predictions

786. The exodus of male priests out of the Catholic church will necessitate the initiation of celibate female priests.

JOHN HOGUE AND VARIOUS CATHOLIC
OBSERVERS

787. They'll [women of the future] ride astride with brazen brow,
     As witches do on broomsticks now.
     Then love shall die and marriage cease,
     And nations wane as babes decrease.
     And wives shall fondle cats and dogs
     And men live much the same as hogs.

MOTHER SHIPTON (C. 1561)

Women riding astride horses was unthinkable in Shipton's time. Currently Russia and some European countries are experiencing fewer births than deaths annually. Modern society obsesses over pets more than any other in the past.

788. The "Aquarian" or "New Age" has also been set down as the period when woman, in the order of upheaval, revolution, and change, would appear on the world's stage in a completely new role. . . .

Women have to come to the front in all matters of public life. I have no hesitation in saying that there is no body of men who will be able for long to resist the tide of thought that for either good or evil is bringing women into power.

CHEIRO (1926)
Cheiro's World Predictions

FASHION

789. And now a word in uncouth rhyme
Of what shall be in future time:
For in these wondrous far-off days,
The women shall adopt a craze
To dress like men and trousers wear,
And cut off their locks of hair.

MOTHER SHIPTON (C. 1561)

790. The fashions of the 2030s will look like a cross between Edwardian-*H.M.S. Titanic* attire and the desert burnooses and costumes from Frank Herbert's *Dune*. Broad Gibson girl hats will also return, and why? The coming UV radiation plague bombarding the earth during the coming era of the ozone holes will require the fashion and health conscious to go retro-Victorian. Indeed the exposure of a little ankle flesh, albeit sunburned if exposed too long, will once again titillate the average retro-Victorian male, perhaps to the point of risking a little retina burn to peek over his UV sunglasses.

JOHN HOGUE (1989)

791. Women and men of the latter-day twentieth century, prepare ye for the Bozo look. Clown clothes and makeup will be en vogue after the 2050s. Men and women today shave their temples, but the stylistic men and women of tomorrow will grow their temple hair long and shave their pates. They will dye their hair rusty red, tease it, and use hairspray to hold it out in horizontal flaming bangs.

792. In the twenty-second century, when people are no longer sexually uptight, daring stylists will adopt the Minoan look. Women will cover everything from head to foot and wear a veil, but their breasts will hang fully exposed.

793. People of the 2090s will appreciate the sacredness of the absurd. Men and women attending peace conferences and corporate meetings alike will want to wear clamp-on, bouncing bug antennae on their heads to keep the meetings light.

JOHN HOGUE (1983)

BEYOND THE NUCLEAR FAMILY

The icon of the two-parent, two-kid family may go the way of nationalism. The Aquarian Age rules mass movements, so it is possible that a more communal family unit may come forth. Are we ready for ancient-future tribalism? Will it take a "global" village to teach a child?

The Nuclear Family Fighting a Nuclear War

794. The godly have been swept from the land. Not one upright man remains.

795. All men lie in wait to shed blood; each hunts his brother with a net. Both hands are skilled in doing evil: the ruler demands gifts, the judge accepts bribes, the powerful dictate what they desire; they all conspire together.

796. The best of them is like a brier, the most upright worse than a thorn hedge.

797. The day of your watchmen has come, the day God visits you. Now is the time of their confusion. Do not trust a neighbor; put no confidence in a friend. Even with her who lies in your embrace be careful of your words. For a son dishonors his father, a daughter rises up against her mother, a daughter-in-law against her mother-in-law. A man's enemies are the members of his own household. But as for me, I watch in hope of the Lord.

MICAH (C. 721 B.C.) *Mic. 7:2–7*

798. The punks and the skinheads are simply reminders that you have failed. The Western civilization has come to its end. Naturally it is always the youth who are most vulnerable to what is coming.

Those people [the punks] are not strange phenomena: you [the parents] are a strange phenomenon. . . . They are simply revolting against you, and it will be good to listen to them. . . . I am all in sympathy for those people; I would like to meet them. I will have immediate rapport with them because I can understand their misery, their anguish. They may prove your saviors. Don't laugh at them, laugh at yourself. They are your children, you have produced them—you must take the responsibility. . . . A tree is known by its fruits. . . . You are the tree—and those insane-looking young people are the fruits. Somewhere you are responsible. They are a question mark on you. Think about them sympathetically. . . .

Unless you understand that the West is in urgent need of a new way of life, more and more outrageous reactions will be there around you, and you will be responsible for it.

OSHO (1986) Socrates Poisoned Again

799. Marriage will no longer be considered a religious rite. It will be a civil contract which will allow a change of partners whenever the contracting couple mutually agrees to separate.

DAVID GOODMAN CROLY (1888)
Glimpses of the Future

800. I'm not saying that all families will disappear. Only spiritual families will remain; nonspiritual families will disappear. . . . Life will be more liquid, more trusting. There will be more trust in the mysteries of life than in the clarities of the law . . . the court, the police, the priests of the Church.

OSHO (1977)

The Communal Family

801. It is also understood, comprehended by some, that if a new order of conditions is to arise, there must be a purging in high places as well as low: and that there must be a greater consideration of the individual, so that each soul being will be his brother's keeper. Then certain circumstances will come about in the political, the economic, and whole relationships in which a leveling will occur . . . or a greater comprehension of the need for it.

EDGAR CAYCE (1938) *No. 3976–18*

802. And with the family disappearing, nations will disappear because the family is the unit of the nation.

OSHO (1987) The Greatest Challenge

803. No more will treacherous gold and silver be
Nor earthly wealth, nor toilsome servitude,
But one fast friendship and one mode of life
Will be with the glad people, and all things
Will common be, and equal light of life.

Sibylline Oracles *(second century B.C.)*

804. The whole world should be one humanity, only divided by small communes on a practical basis. No fanaticism, no racism, no nationalism—then, for the first time, we can drop the idea of wars. We can make life with honesty, worth living, worth enjoying—playful, meditative, creative—and give every man and every woman equal opportunity to grow and bring their potential to flowering.

OSHO (1987) The Greatest Challenge

805. For changes are coming, this may be sure—an evolution, or revolution in the ideas of religious thought. The *basis* of it for the world will eventually come out of Russia; not Communism, no! But rather that which is the basis of the same, as the Christ taught—His kind of communism!

EDGAR CAYCE (C. 1930) No. 452–6

THE DARKER SIDE OF THE GOLDEN "AQUARIAN" AGE

In predictive astrology every potential destiny has a dark and a light side. The next twenty centuries of the Aquarian Age will either see everyone as equally unique and the World State existing to nurture an individual's uniqueness to his or her full potential, or it will see everyone as mentally, physically, and genetically programmed to serve the World State, which exists to control the mind and feelings of the individual and impart an artificial sense of achieving his or her full potential.

806. What Fukuyama is saying [in his "end of history" theory] is absolutely baseless. History moves in waves—there will again be something like Fascism arising in the world.

OSHO (1989)

807. As we pass the cosmic border from Pisces to Aquarius our own tumultuous age has been foreseen as one of materialistic degeneration and maximum destruction especially at its beginning, which is now.

CHARLES BERLITZ (1981)

808. Man cannot find any meaning in life, so he becomes a victim of a utopian life in the future, and by taking away his future you are turning him into a robot. . . . What Fukuyama is saying is more dangerous to humanity than anything [said] by Stalin, or Mussolini, or Hitler!

OSHO (1989)

809. Never before in world history has there been such potential for a few wrong-minded people to control the masses.

810. There is real danger of a few evil people slipping into these positions [of power] in order to disrupt important work and governmental economies, or to control universal thought and action.

SPIRIT GUIDES OF RUTH MONTGOMERY
(1985) Aliens Among Us

811. A machine can easily be made by which one man can draw a thousand to himself by violence against their wills and attract other things in like manner.

ROGER BACON (1268)

812. In a certain way television has introduced a new kind of primitiveness.

OSHO (1987) Om Mani Padme Hum

813. Nothing will be holy anymore. Everything will be upset. The great clearance will commence. All states will be pitted against each other. The free life and thought will be imprisoned and banished. Severe masters will rule and will try to get everything under their discipline. It will be a terrible time.

STORMBERGER (EIGHTEENTH CENTURY)

814. Right now you have memories; soon you won't have. Everybody will be carrying his own computer . . . carried in the pocket and which can contain all the knowledge contained in the libraries of the world—you just have to know how to make it function. Man will fall tremendously as far as intelligence is concerned, memory is concerned. Everything that comes into existence brings changes so silently you don't see them.

OSHO (1987) Om Mani Padme Hum

815. The business world will be in the hands of a few great firms which will control the wealth of many nations.

DAVID GOODMAN CROLY (1888)
Glimpses of the Future

816. Tendencies in the hearts and souls of men are such that these may be brought about. For, as indicated through these channels oft, it is not the world, the earth, the environs about it nor the planetary influences, nor the associations or activities, that RULE man. RATHER does man by HIS COMPLIANCE with divine law—bring ORDER out of chaos; or, by his DISREGARD of the associations and laws of the divine influence, bring chaos and DESTRUCTIVE forces into his experience.

EDGAR CAYCE (1935) *No. 416–7*

817. Yea, to be sure, America may boast, but rather is that principle [of freedom] being forgotten . . . that is the sin of America.

EDGAR CAYCE (1944) *No. 3976–29*

818. Never before in world history has there been such potential for a few wrong-minded people to control the masses; yet never has there been so much potential for good if right-thinking, peace-loving people are there to direct the machines that will be "read" daily by many millions in schools offices and homes. Lives will be saved, time conserved, and a new lifestyle emerge as people take their informational readouts from computers.

SPIRIT GUIDES OF RUTH MONTGOMERY
(1985) Aliens Among Us

THE COMING DEATH OF PAST TRADITIONS

819. What is rotten will fall, never to rise again.

THIRD SECRET OF FA'TIMA (1917),
ATTRIBUTED TO THE VIRGIN MARY

820. This—the inward and outward fulfillment, the finality, that awaits every living Culture—is the purport of all the historic "declines." Amongst them is that decline of the Classical which we know so well and fully. Another decline, entirely comparable to it in course and duration, will occupy the first centuries of the coming millennium, and is heralded already and sensibly in and around us today—the decline of the West.

OSWALD SPENGLER (1926)
The Decline of the West

821. By their fruit you will recognize them. . . . A good tree cannot bear bad fruit, and a bad tree cannot bear good fruit. Every tree that does not bear good fruit is cut down and thrown into the fire. Thus, by their fruit you will recognize them.

JESUS CHRIST (a.d. 30–33) *Matt. 7:16–20*

822. Furthermore, not only have these sacrilegious beings gradually distorted for their egoistic and political aims the teachings of the Divine Teacher, but they have now begun to destroy the memory of it.

G. I. GURDJIEFF (1924–27)

Beelzebub's Tales to His Grandson

823. Even if the whole world disappears [nations and organized religions], politicians will be prepared to accept that, but they will not be ready to surrender all of their arms, all of their armies to a world organization.

OSHO (1987) The Greatest Challenge

824. Religious, racial, national, and political bias: all these prejudices strike at the very root of human life; one and all they beget bloodshed, and the ruination of the world. So long as these prejudices survive, there will be continuous and fearsome wars.

'ABDU'L-BAHÁ (C. 1920) Selections

825. For then there will be great distress, unequaled from the beginning of the world until now—and never equaled again. If those days had not been cut short, no one would survive, but for the sake of the elect those days will be shortened.

JESUS CHRIST (a.d. 30–33) *Matt. 24:21–22*

826. If we are going to solve the problems of the future and dissolve them, then we have to look for their roots in the past. . . .

We have to take a quantum leap and teach the new generation not to live the way we have lived. Only then can the future be changed.

OSHO (1987) The Greatest Challenge

827. Until we all Awaken to the Situation and purpose of human existence, we will create no lasting peace or order, and each day will bring the world closer to the finite chaos of War and Bewilderment. But if the Wisdom of the true Spiritual Adepts is "heard" in the human world, then the true revolution can begin, and all dreadful destiny that now lies before us can be dissolved in the Heart of God.

AVATAR ADI DA SAMRAJ (1979)
Scientific Proof of the Existence
of God . . .

828. The "old" is about to give birth to the "new." In all lands, in all peoples, the "travail pains" are becoming more and more intense. The last War [World War I] was but "the turning in the womb" of Nature; the real birth has yet to come. Alack and alas, to those who must cling to the "old"; to the traditions of the past, to the habits of their forebears—their day has already passed forever.

829. The clock of Time has struck the "Midnight Hour"; the blackest darkness lies before the greatest dawn.

The cry "O Lord, how long—how long?" will break from many hearts before the light of the new civilization will chase away the shadows of the night.

CHEIRO (1926)
Cheiro's World Predictions

830. The most important need of humanity today is to be made aware that its past has betrayed it; that there is no point in continuing the past—it will be suicidal—and that a new humanity is absolutely and urgently needed.

OSHO (1987)
The Greatest Challenge

A SHIFT IN CONSCIOUSNESS

Nothing exists in a vacuum. If hallowed traditions die with their age, a new set of traditions will come to replace them.

831. The Heart of the World Is Broken, yet it Rises anew—I Cannot Understand It.

MADAME SYLVIA (1948)

832. Again and again between these catastrophes of blood and terror the cry rises up for reconciliation of the peoples and for peace on earth.

OSWALD SPENGLER (1926)
The Decline of the West

833. After the purification of the world, men will again love each other, as they have previously hated each other. It will be a glorious age. Great preachers and holy men will appear and perform miracles.

MATHIAS LANG (1820)

834. Not only the purification of the human body, but a worldwide purification in every field is impending. This means a general housecleaning of the whole world and the obliteration of the clouds of negativity accumulated during thousands of years.

MEISHU-SAMA (1955)

○　○　○　○　○　○

THE PRESENT-DAY RELIGIONS PASS AWAY

○　○　○　○　○　○

The Age of Pisces began two thousand years ago with the rise of Christianity. At its inception, the new religion crowded out the mainstream religions of Isis and Mithras. Today a new era is dawning. Could it be that we will experience the eclipse of some or all of the current mainstream religions that have dominated the dying age of Pisces?

THE END OF TODAY'S MAINSTREAM RELIGIONS

835. Behold the days come, saith the Lord, and I will send forth a famine into the land: not a famine of bread, nor a thirst of water, but of hearing the word of the Lord. And they shall move from sea to sea, and from the north to the east: they shall go about seeking the word of the Lord, and shall not find it. In that day the fair virgins, and the young men shall faint for thirst:

AMOS (C. 750 B.C.) *Amos 8:11–13*

836. And the great monarch of the world [the messiah] will create new laws for the new mankind and will cause a new age to begin, in which there will be only one flock and one shepherd, and peace will be of long, long duration, for the glory of God in heaven and on earth.

> PASTOR BARTHOLOMAEUS
> HOLZHAUSER (C. 1642)

837. The cycle of Pisces, nearly two thousand years ago, ushered in the dawn of Christianity. Its period in the Precession of the Equinox is two thousand one hundred and fifty years—*it has nearly run its course.*

> CHEIRO (1931)
> Cheiro's World Predictions

838. Before us there stands a last spiritual crisis that will involve all Europe and America.

> OSWALD SPENGLER (1926)
> The Decline of the West

839. Oh Egypt, Egypt, of thy religion nothing will remain but an empty tale, which thine own children in time to come will not believe; nothing will be left but graven words, and only the stones will tell of thy piety.

> HERMES TRISMEGISTUS (a.d. 150–270)
> Asclepius III

840. At that time many will turn away from the faith and will betray and hate each other, and many false prophets will appear and deceive many people. Because of the increase of wickedness, the love of most will grow cold, but he who stands firm to the end will be saved. And this gospel of the kingdom will be preached in the whole world as a testimony to all nations, and then the end will come.

JESUS CHRIST (a.d. 30–33)

Matt. 24:10–14

841. Priests and servants of the church will be reduced to misery, the youth led by atheism, and republics will be established in the whole world. And everything will be destroyed by wars.

PASTOR BARTHOLOMAEUS

HOLZHAUSER (C. 1642)

842. The day humanity is completely finished with these exploiters in the name of religion, this very Earth can become a paradise. There is no need to wait for death. What has death to do with paradise? Paradise is the way you live. Paradise has something to do with life, not with death.

OSHO (1985)

From the False to the True

843. Write to your brothers throughout the world, telling them that it is necessary to bring about a reform of both customs and people themselves. If that is not achieved, the bread of the Divine word will not be broken among the people.

ST. JOHN BOSCO (1874)

844. Under the guise of humanity, Religion will creep back to her cradle of poverty and persecution, and in the next hundred years there will be as many religious sects in the World as there are pieces of supposed "true Cross" in existence at the present time.

CHEIRO (1926)
Cheiro's World Predictions

845. Because Christianity and the other major religions are not compatible with scientific knowledge, man will satisfy his emotional/spiritual cravings with art.

DAVID GOODMAN CROLY (1888)
Glimpses of the Future

846. To my way of thinking the greatest mystery of life is— God is so patient that the slow tortoise of evolution moves ever on. Races may die, Empires may fall, cities may crumble, yet something is gained. The upward path may be tedious, the track winding and devious, false guides may lose their way, religions may beckon and vanish, but the upward urge remains.

CHEIRO (1926)
Cheiro's World Predictions

847. If religiousness spreads all over the world, the religions will fade away. It will be a tremendous blessing to humanity when man is simply man, neither Christian, nor Mohammedan, nor Hindu. . . . Only then will there be a peace that passeth all mis-understanding.

OSHO (1987)
The Greatest Challenge

CATHOLICISM

Two Popes Left to Rule Before Judgment Day

848. Either John Paul II or his successor will be compelled to make Mary, mother of Jesus Christ, co-redeemer to her son.

JOHN HOGUE (1998) *The Last Pope*

849. The successor [to John Paul II] will be Pope *Gloria Olivae*—"Glory of the Olive."

PROPHECY OF ST. MALACHY (C. 1140)

850. Not from Spain, but from ancient France, will be elected for the trembling ship [the papacy]. He will make a promise to the enemy who will cause great plague during his reign.

NOSTRADAMUS (1555) *C5 Q49*

Cardinal Lustiger of France, an important candidate to succeed John Paul II, is the Archbishop of Paris.

851. The next pope after John Paul II will die and be replaced in 2008.

JOHN HOGUE (1998) *The Last Pope*

852. This pope [John Paul's sucessor] will take Leo XVI for his name and will be an agent of peace between Israelis and Arabs [the olive is also a symbol of Israel].

A PADUAN PROPHET-MONK

(EIGHTEENTH CENTURY)

853. During the last persecution of the Holy Roman Church, there shall sit *Petrus Romanus* [Peter of Rome], who shall feed the sheep amid great tribulations, and when these have passed, the City of the Seven Hills shall be utterly destroyed, and the awful Judge will judge the people.

PROPHECY OF ST. MALACHY (C. 1140)

854. I had a horrible vision. Was it of me or one of my successors? I saw the Pope leaving Rome and, to get out of the Vatican, he had to step over the corpses of his priests.

POPE PIUS X (1909)

Scandals and Schisms to Come

855. The time is coming when princes and peoples will reject the authority of the Pope. Some countries will prefer their own Church leaders to the Pope.

HILDEGARD VON BINGEN (C. 1141)

856. Mount Aventine [Rome] will be seen to burn at night. . . . The heavens obscured very suddenly in Flanders [great solar eclipse in 1999]:. . .

Then Church people will commit the scandals.

NOSTRADAMUS (1555) *C3 Q17*

The Vatican will suffer a new scandal in 2000 after a solar eclipse in August of 1999.

857. In the sacred temples scandals will be committed. They will be thought of as honors and praiseworthy. Of one of whom they engrave on silver, gold and medals [the pope]. The end will be very strange torments.

NOSTRADAMUS (1555) *C6 Q9*

858. Of the Church people blood will be poured out in as great abundance as water: And for a long time it will not be suppressed. Woe, woe for the clergy ruin and grief.

NOSTRADAMUS (1555) *C8 Q98*

This could indicate future persecution of the Roman Catholic Clergy.

859. Even "the Church" will have revolution within itself. Strange creeds will be preached from all pulpits.

CHEIRO (1926)
Cheiro's World Predictions

860. For a time Religion will save itself from catastrophe by abolishing its Bishops' "palaces," its gilded ceremonials, and its alliance with Monarchs. State and Church will separate and will cease backing up one another.

CHEIRO (1926)
Cheiro's World Predictions

861. The profession which will be topmost in this business of AIDS will be the priests, the nuns, the monks . . . because they have been practicing perverted sex longer than anybody else.

OSHO (1985)
From Misery to Enlightenment

862. The church will suffer great ills; a torrent of evil will open a breach on her, but the first attack will be against her fortune and her riches [Vatican Bank scandal?].

RAVIGNAN (1847), A JESUIT PRIEST

The Vatican and Rome Are Destroyed by Fires and Floods

863. Very near the Tiber death threatens, shortly after the great flood. The pope will be taken prisoner and cast out, the castle [St. Angelo] and the Palace [Vatican] in flames.

NOSTRADAMUS (1555) C2 Q93

864. A torrent to open the tomb of marble and lead to the great Roman with the Mendusine Device.

NOSTRADAMUS (1557) C9 Q84

In the spring of the year 2000 the tomb of St. Peter will be uncovered in the ruins of the Vatican after the flood. The "Great Roman" is interpreted as St. Peter, since "Mendusine" is an anagram for "Deus in Me," Peter's motto. St. Malachy also calls the last pope Peter.

The Catholic Apocalypse

865. And if humanity opposes me, I shall be obliged to free the arm of My Son. Now I see that God will punish man with a severity that has not been used since the Flood.

866. The time of times will come and everything will come to an end if humanity is not converted, and if things remain as they are now or get worse, or get very much worse, the great and powerful men will perish just as will the small and weak.

867. For the Church, too, the time of its greatest trial will come. Cardinals will oppose cardinals and bishops [will be] against bishops. Satan will march in their midst and there will be great changes at Rome.

868. The church will be darkened and the world will shake with terror.

869. The unexpected will follow [a great war] in every part of the world, anxiety, pain, and misery in every country.

870. The time is getting ever nearer and the abyss is getting wider without hope. The good will perish with the bad, the great with the small, the Heads of the Church with their faithful, and the rulers with their people.

871. There will be death everywhere as a result of the mistakes of the unfeeling and the partisans of Satan, but when those who survive all these happenings are still alive, they will proclaim God again and His Glory, and will serve him as in the time when the world was not so perverted.

ATTRIBUTED TO THE THIRD SECRET OF
FA'TIMA (1917)

872. Joachim de Fiore, a Calabrian Abbott of the 12ᵗʰ century foresaw Christianity evolving in three ages. The age of the father [Old Testament era], the age of the Son [the twenty centuries of Jesus Christ's mission leading up to the year 2000], and the age of the Holy Spirit.

873. The Church of Rome shall be destroyed in the Third [age of the Holy Spirit], as the Synagogue of the Jews was destroyed in the Second [age of the Son—Christ], and the spiritual church shall from thenceforth succeed, to the end of the world.

874. The Third [the age of the Holy Spirit] therefore will be ushered in toward the close of the present age, no longer under the screen of the letter, but in the spirit of complete freedom.

JOACHIM DE FIORE (TWELFTH CENTURY)

In the final stage it could be interpreted that humanity will have a direct relationship with the divine and will not need a priesthood as mediator.

PROTESTANT CHRISTIAN SECTS

875. The Protestants will be entirely undone in all of Europe and part of Africa by the Islamics.

NOSTRADAMUS (1557)
Epistle to Henry II

JUDAISM

876. Calamity upon calamity will come, and rumor upon rumor. They will try to get a vision from the prophet; the teaching of the law by the priest will be lost, as will the counsel of the elders.

EZEKIEL (593–571 B.C.) *Ezek.* 7:26

877. The religion founded on the teaching of St. Moses, although it existed for a long time and is still maintained after a fashion by its followers, yet, owing to the organic hatred formed in the beings of other communities toward the beings who follow their religion, due only to that "maleficent" idea called "policy," infallibly sooner or later they will doubtlessly "croak it" as well and also "with a crash."

G. I. GURDJIEFF (1924–27)
Beelzebub's Tales to His Grandson

ISLAM

878. Islam will fall after a man walks on the lamp of the night [the Moon].

ATTRIBUTED TO MUHAMMAD (A.D. 620–30)

879. Men will increasingly neglect their souls. . . . The greatest corruption will reign on earth. Men will become like bloodthirsty animals, thirsting for the blood of their brothers. The crescent [Islam] will become obscured and its followers will descend into lies and perpetual warfare.

ARGHATI PROPHECY (CENTURIES AGO)

880. Of course, by the destruction in Turkey of this "dervishism" [the Sufis] those last dying sparks will also be entirely extinguished there which, preserved as it were in the ashes, might sometime rekindle the hearth of those possibilities upon which St. Muhammad counted and which he had hoped.

G. I. GURDJIEFF (1924–27)
Beelzebub's Tales to His Grandson

HINDUISM

881. Whenever there is noticed an increase [in the number] of heretics, then . . . should the full swing of Kali [the darkest, most apocalyptic age] be estimated by the wise. When the people do not show respect to the sayings of the Vedas, but are inclined toward the heretics, then . . . the augmented influence of the Kali age should be inferred.

Vishnu Purana *(c. A.D. 500)*, 6:1, 44–47

Hinduism may end when:

882. Wealth will be the only source of devotion.

883. Passion will be the sole bond of union between the sexes. Falsehood will be the only means of success in litigation. Women will be objects merely of sensual gratification.

Vishnu Purana *(c. A.D. 900)*, 4

BUDDHISM

884. The holders of the faith, the glorious rebirths, will be broken down and left without a name. As regards the monasteries and the priesthood, their lands and other properties will be destroyed.

THIRTEENTH DALAI LAMA OF TIBET
(1932) *Final Declaration*

885. Most probably I am the last [Dalai Lama]. Nothing wrong. When there is no longer any benefit, then naturally the Dalai Lama ceases to be.

FOURTEENTH DALAI LAMA OF TIBET (C.
1980)

SHAMANIST AND ANIMIST FAITHS

886. When holy metals are dug out of Mt. Isa, the end is near.

ANCIENT ABORIGINAL PROPHECY

White Australians currently mine uranium from Mt. Isa, Queensland.

887. If we dig precious things from the land we will perish.

HOPI INDIANS OF NORTH AMERICA

Uranium mining on Hopi lands continues unabated.

○ ○ ○ ○ ○ ○

THE NEW RELIGIONS

○ ○ ○ ○ ○

Religions of faith dominated the Piscean Age; however, religions rooted in science are expected to dominate the Aquarian Age.

SPIRITUAL REVOLUTION IN THE TWENTY-FIRST CENTURY

888. There comes a moment where reason fails, where the absurd, the irrational, the mystical, the miraculous, raises its head. The coming one hundred years are going to be more and more irrational. I do not ordinarily make prophecies, but about this I am absolutely prophetic: the coming one hundred years are going to be more and more irrational, and more and more mystical.

OSHO (1986) Osho Upanishad

889. The next twenty years [1978–99] are crucial to the unfolding of a soul's spiritual being, for unless mankind uses these years to smooth out past karma and prepare for the spirit state, the opportunities may not come again for thousands of years, inasmuch as the human population will be decimated and opportunities for entering physical bodies will be slim.

Those who strive now to complete their rehabilitation will advance more rapidly in spirit, to compensate for the lost opportunities in the Earth life.

SPIRIT GUIDES OF RUTH MONTGOMERY
(1979) Strangers Among Us

890. The time is very short. . . . So much destructive force is accumulating that unless a few individuals gather courage and revolt against all that is past . . . I am not telling you to choose, to choose that which is good and to leave that which is bad. They are all together; you cannot do that. The past has to be simply erased, as if we are for the first time on the earth and there has been no history. That is the only possibility to create a beautiful world full of love, full of fragrance, with deep respect for everybody. The past has lived centered on hate. The future can live only if it is centered on love. The past has been unconscious. The future can only be conscious. . . . We can either die with the past or be reborn with the future.

OSHO (1987) Om Mani Padme Hum

891. Let the future disclose the hour when the Brides of inner meaning will, as decreed by the Will of God, hasten forth, unveiled, out of their mystic mansions, and manifest themselves in the ancient realm of beings.

BAHÁ'U'LLÁH (1853) Kitab-i-Iqan

892. I want therefore to set man free, rejoicing as the bird in the clear sky, unburdened, independent, ecstatic, in that freedom.

J. Krishnamurti (1929)
Truth Is a Pathless Land

Religionless Religion

893. Once you have tasted your own immortality, you start spreading an invisible fire. . . . People will be immensely touched by your presence, by your aroma, by your fragrance, by your love. We need in the world more love to balance war.

894. Forget doing, grow into your being. And the growth of your being is contagious; it will help many people to light their unlit torches from your life fire. . . . Politicians will be left alone without any support from their armies, from their scientists, from their intelligentsia, from mystics, from poets. And against all this intelligence, all their nuclear weapons will become impotent. They can create war only if unconsciously we are ready to commit suicide, if in some way we are supportive to them. It is our support that has given them power. If we withdraw our support, their power disappears. They didn't have any power of their own.

895. It is a great challenge, a very adventurous time. When the world is facing suicide, the possibility is that the world can be convinced—not intellectually but through your growing hearts, your love—to let the old world die and the new world with new values be born. You won't have such an opportunity again. In the past there was never such an opportunity. It is not to be missed.

OSHO (1987) The New Dawn

896. Such perfection cannot be attained until all religions have become merged into one. This, the apparently "impossible," is every day becoming more and more probable. The sway and power of State-supported creeds is on the decline, or splitting into so many sects that they are "like sheep without a shepherd."

CHEIRO (1931)
Cheiro's World Predictions

The Religious Axis Shift: The Eastern Religions Flower in the West

897. The new epoch will deliver you from speech, because you will be able to feel what is in the thoughts of other men.

MADAME SYLVIA (1948)

898. The man from the East will come.

NOSTRADAMUS (1555) C2 Q29

899. He will appear in Asia, at home in Europe.

NOSTRADAMUS (1557) C10 Q75

900. You have to understand: in those far mountains of the East rests the secret power. It will inexorably extend over the whole Earth and will tower toward the sky.

901. Everything that recalls the old times will collapse. Soon you will face a new world, new conceptions of the world, new organizations, new laws.

MADAME SYLVIA (1948)

When the founder of Tibetan Buddhism, the guru Padmasam-bhava, bade farewell to his disciples twelve centuries ago, it was with a parting prophecy:

902. When the iron bird flies and horses run on wheels, the Tibetan people will be scattered like ants across the face of the Earth, and the Dharma will come to the land of the red men.

PADMASAMBHAVA

MEDITATION, THE NEW RELIGIOUS SCIENCE

Science in the Aquarian Age will evolve into two wings: the objective and the subjective (the science of knowing the knower).

Objective Science Balanced by Subjective Science

903. Science will be for making life more comfortable, more conscious, more beautiful; and meditation will become an absolute part of education all over the world. And the balance between [science and meditation] will create the whole man. Without meditation you cannot have the clarity, and a grounding within yourself, and a vision which is simple and innocent. . . . This synthesis can create a totally new science.

OSHO (1987) The Greatest Challenge

904. This much we know: the two dimensions of spirit and physical being will become as one when universal law is more fully grasped. Feel the kinship with all of God's creations, and strive for that which is just. Banish fears, abolish angers, and work for the common good.

SPIRIT GUIDES OF RUTH MONTGOMERY
(1976) The World Before

At the onset of the most scientific and technologically dominated century, 'Abdu'l-Bahá predicted a successful synthesis of the spiritual and material sciences in the near future:

905. This union will bring about true civilization where the spiritual is expressed and carried out in the material. Receiving thus, the one from the other, the greatest harmony will prevail, all people will be united, a state of great perfection will be attained, there will be a firm cementing, and this world will become a shining mirror for the reflection of the attributes of God.

'ABDU'L-BAHÁ (1911) Paris Talks

Psychologists Replaced by the Psychology of the Buddhas

906. Within fifty years for the first time psychology will be really born. Freudian psychology is very primitive; it is like an aboriginal religion compared to Buddha.

After a hundred years it will simply look silly. These people who are working in encounter, psychodrama, bioenergetics, gestalt, and others . . . their work is to contribute, to pool all that is possible from every direction, and once the real psychology will start taking shape, they will start to disappear.

OSHO (1976)

The Sound of Running Water

907. Utopia *is* possible. It is only a question of understanding the value of meditation.

OSHO (1989)

Deprogramming People from Being So Predictable

908. The day of your watchmen has come, the day God visits you.

MICAH (C. 721 b.c.) *Mic. 7:4*

909. But your dead will live; their bodies will rise. You who dwell in the dust, wake up and shout for joy. Your dew is like the dew of the morning; the earth will give birth to her dead.

ISAIAH (738–687 b.c.) *Isa. 26:19*

Osho defined the coming spiritual rebellion as a manifesto of silence:

910. Silence means: inside you, you are just spaciousness, uncluttered spaciousness. Silence means you have put aside the whole furniture of the mind—the thoughts, the desires, the memories, the fantasies, the dreams—all you have pushed aside. You are just looking into existence directly, immediately. You are in contact with existence without anything in between you and existence. . . . A tremendous transformation is needed to hear silence and to understand silence. Silence is the basic requirement for understanding God, the basic requirement to know Truth.

OSHO (1980)
The Wild Geese and the Water

911. Then will the eyes of the blind be opened and the ears of the deaf unstopped.

ISAIAH (738–687 B.C.) *Isa. 35:5*

912. [To] those then, that are come into the new life, the new understanding—the new regeneration there *is* then the new Jerusalem . . . not a place, alone, but as a condition, as an experience of the soul.

EDGAR CAYCE (D. 1945) *No. 281–37*

913. The church is within yourself and not in any pope nor preacher, nor in any building but in self. For thy body is indeed the temple of the living God and the Christ becomes a personal companion in mind and in body.

EDGAR CAYCE (1944) *No. 5125–1*

914. Man will have to change within himself, not try to change others, in order to prevent wars.

SPIRIT GUIDES OF RUTH MONTGOMERY
(1979) Strangers Among Us

915. The mistrust of the human being towards herself and everyone else is her greatest ball and chain anklet. . . . She trudges under great strain. She is pulling herself around with her mistrust, with her inherited world of images from unlimited generations back in time. I want to say that if she would only look down on her burden and start to watch it closely, she would find that the strong metal chains are really only a thread as thin as a spider web and that her iron ball is only a red balloon.

AMBRES (1986)

916. The spiritual revolution can be reduced to a simple maxim: You disappear and let God be.

OSHO (1987) The Rebellious Spirit

○ ○ ○ ○ ○ ○

A NEW HUMANITY

○ ○ ○ ○ ○ ○

The minority prophetic view down through the ages points to the coming century of the new millennium as the seeding ground for a true and mystic revolution. The catalyst for this creative apocalypse is a new breed of human being who is spiritually rebellious.

These early members of the species Homo novus ("the new man") will give birth to a fearless humanity, liberated from past and future obsessions, who will live with alertness, creativity, and delight in the present moment. They will spread and establish a global society that can work together to make a world so rich in health, technology, and luxury that all individuals are free to discover and live their uniqueness to the fullest.

TRADITIONALLY ANTI-LIFE HUMANITY

917. The old man, the way he has existed for centuries, is afraid of life—not afraid of death. Death, he worships; life he renounces.

OSHO (1987) The Golden Future

918. A peculiar generation now exists on this Earth, which does not carry an urge for inner growth, but only death for the whole race. And someday, at some future time, people will say: there lived a clan and here and there again—Germans, Britons, or Franks—the old, eternal law induced them to dig their own graves. They are digging graves also for their own souls. Britons, Franks, or Germans or whatever the country where they live: they are all united by an old law, which provides that they wither and die. When the sun will again rise over the graves in golden glory, a new generation will arise in the course of time and a new mankind.

SEERESS REGINA (EARLY TWENTIETH CENTURY)

919. The old man was basically taught to be a hypocrite; the greater hypocrite he was, the more honored, the more rewarded . . . because he had settled with society.

OSHO (1987) The Greatest Challenge

920. A man who strays from the path of understanding comes to rest in the company of the dead.

Prov. 21:16

921. The old man is determined to die, committed to suicide. Let him die peacefully.

OSHO (1987)
From Death to Deathlessness

HOMO NOVUS: THE NEW HUMANITY

922. O Force-compelled, Fate-driven Earth-born race,
O petty adventurers in an infinite world
And prisoners of a dwarf humanity,
How long will you tread the circling tracts of mind
Around your little self and petty things?
But not for a changeless littleness were you meant,
Not for vain repetition were you built . . .
Almighty powers are shut in nature's cells.
A greater destiny awaits you in your front . . .
The life you lead conceals the light you are.

SRI AUROBINDO (1946–48) Savitri

923. Those who really desire to understand, who are looking to find that which is eternal, without beginning and without an end, will walk together with a greater intensity, will be a danger to everything that is unessential, to unrealities, to shadows. And they will concentrate, they will become the flame, because they understand.

J. KRISHNAMURTI (1929)
Truth Is a Pathless Land

924. I saw the sun-eyed children of a marvelous dawn . . .
The massive barrier-breakers of the world . . .
The architects of immortality . . .
Bodies made beautiful by the 'spirit's light,
Carrying the magic word, the mystic fire,
Carrying the Dionysian cup of joy.

SRI AUROBINDO (1946–47) Savitri

925. Even now, under our very eyes, the new Race and races are preparing to be formed, and it is in America that the transformation will take place.

Thus it is the mankind of the New World . . . whose mission and Karma it is to sow the seeds for a forthcoming grander, and far more glorious Race than any of those we know of at present. The cycles of matter will be succeeded by the cycles of Spirituality and a fully developed mind.

H. B. BLAVATSKY (1888)
The Secret Doctrine, *vol. 3*

926. A new world is born. At present we are right in the midst of a transitional period in which the two are mingled: The old world persists, yet all-powerful, continuing to dominate the ordinary consciousness, and the new one slips in quietly . . . unobserved to the extent that externally it changes little for the moment. . . . And yet it works, it grows, till one day it will be sufficiently strong to impose itself visibly.

THE MOTHER (1931) Conversations

927. Man is also a new stage in the event of time. His newness or uniqueness is hidden. This higher brain is the structural cauldron of the present and future evolutionary changes of Man and what is beyond Man in the scheme of the World.

AVATAR ADI DA SAMRAJ (1978)
The Enlightenment of the Whole Body

928. [The new race] will silently come into existence . . . the peculiar children who will grow into peculiar men and women—will be regarded as abnormal oddities, physically and mentally. Then, as they increase, and the numbers become with every age greater, one day they will awake to find themselves in a majority. Then present men will begin to be regarded as exceptional mongrels, until they die out in their turn in civilized lands.

H. B. BLAVATSKY (1888)
The Secret Doctrine, *vol. 3*

929. The most important need of humanity today is to be made aware that its past has betrayed it; that there is no point in continuing the past—it will be suicidal—that a new humanity is absolutely and urgently needed. And the new humanity will not be a society in the old sense, where individuals are only parts of it.

930. The new humanity will be a meeting of individuals, where individuals are the masters, and society is to serve them. It will have many different aspects to it. It will not have so many religions, it will have only a religious consciousness. It will not have a despot God as a creator, because that implies the slavery of man. It will have godliness as a quality of ultimate achievement—a quality of enlightenment. God will be spread all over—in everything, in every being.

931. The individual, for the first time, will not be programmed; he will be helped to be himself. He will not be given any ideals, any discipline, any certain pattern; he will be given only a tremendous love for freedom, so that he can sacrifice everything—even his own life—but he cannot sacrifice freedom.

932. The new individual will not be repressive; he will be natural, with no inhibitions, expressive of everything that he has; just the way plants express themselves in different colors, in different fragrances, each individual will be doing the same.

933. The new individual will not have the false idea that all human beings are equal. They are not—they are unique, which is a far superior concept than equality. Although the new individuals will not be equal, they will have equal opportunity to grow into their potential, whatever it is.

934. There will be no marriage; love will be the only law. Children will be part of the commune, and only the commune will decide who is capable of being a mother and who is capable of being a father. It cannot be at random and accidental. And it will be according to the needs of the Earth.

935. The new humanity will have an ecology in which nature is not to be conquered, but lived and loved. We are part of it—how can we conquer it? It will not have races, no distinctions between nations, between colors, casts. It will not have any nations, and states; it will have only a functional world government.

936. The new man is an absolute necessity. The old is dead or is dying . . . cannot survive long. And if we cannot produce a new human being, then humanity will disappear from the Earth.

OSHO (1986) Beyond Psychology

937. It is hoping against hope—but I still hope that the danger of global death will be the shock which awakens humanity. If man survives after this century, it will be a new man and a new humanity. One thing is certain: Either man has to die or man has to change. I cannot think that man will chose to die.

938. The longing for life is so great. . . . Just to think that the Earth has become dead—no trees, no humanity, no birds, no animals . . . it is such a great crisis. . . . And if the third world war does not happen, that will mean a great change, a tidal change in human consciousness. We will see a new man.

OSHO (1987) The New Dawn

939. In this new Earth, Evil has ended and every ill has ceased. . . . Pure are they, the members of this new race, and without stain. The food they share with one another in time's second morning is honey dew, and their children shall overspread the Earth.

The Ragnarök

This is one of the few hopeful references suggesting there will be a new flow of time. Time will run out for the old man and his archaic ways, but not for humanity as such.

940. All nations should become one in faith, and all men as brothers; that the bonds of affection and unity between the sons of men should be strengthened; that diversity of religion should cease, and differences of race be annulled.

SHOGHI EFFENDI QUOTING
BAHA''U'LLÁH

941. In the future humanity will have a higher consciousness and be able to travel from planet to planet, from galaxy to galaxy by the sole power of the mind.

A SHAMAN FROM THE ANDES (1998)

942. The way of evolution is a long, long road. The school of life has many, many classes. The making of a soul, eons and eons of civilizations.

CHEIRO (1931)
Cheiro's World Predictions

A NEW HEAVEN AND A NEW EARTH

Here are some differing views of what the earthly, post-apocalyptic world will be:

943. Then I saw a new Heaven and a new Earth: for the first heaven and the first Earth had passed away.

ST. JOHN OF PATMOS (a.d. 81–96)
Rev. 21:1

944. Mars and the scepter will be in conjunction [June 21, 2002]. A calamitous war under Cancer [July 1999]. A short time afterward a new king will be anointed who will bring peace to the earth for a long time.

NOSTRADAMUS (1555) *C6 Q24*

945. All manmade progress will be enlisted for destruction. However, the great fate will raise her hand in warning and will command to stop. If men will listen to the judicious ones among them and stop, it will be their advantage; if not, it will be their misfortune, and a great calamity will follow.

PROPHECY OF MONTREAL (1888)

946. Everything will be decided by how we travel over this precipitous passage [in time]. If we survive the trail, carefully traversing it without falling, then everything will be recovered and health will return. But if we miss one step we will fail; the world will remain unhealthy. Man will grievously suffer from the effects or die altogether.

ATTRIBUTED TO DEGUCHI NAO
(C. 1896)

947. Yes, all the predictions of the ancient seers, like Nostradamus, that the world is going to end by the end of this century, are true in a very different sense than it has been understood. . . . The old [humanity] has to disappear to give place to a new man with fresh values: with one Earth undivided into nations, with one humanity undivided by religion. . . . Changes have been happening. They will come to a peak by the end of this century, when the moment of ultimate decision will have to be faced by humanity. Transform yourself totally: drop all that is old, don't look backward. Start creating new values, look forward—because the past is past and to visit the graveyard too much is dangerous. . . . It is the future that should be your concern. It is the future and the faraway stars that will become your challenges.

OSHO (1987) The Greatest Challenge

948. When a night will come and the White Pope and the Black Pope [head of Jesuits or an antipope] die at the same time, then there will dawn upon the Christian nations the Great White Day.

OLD ITALIAN PROPHECY

949. And thou shalt say to them: Thus saith the Lord God: Behold I will take the children of Israel from the midst of the nations whither they are gone: and I will gather them on every side, and will bring them to their own land. And I will make them one nation in the land on the mountains of Israel, and one king shall be king over them all: and they shall no more be two nations, . . . neither shall they be defiled any more with their idols, nor with their abominations, nor with all their iniquities: and I will save them out of all the places in which they have sinned, and I will cleanse them: and they shall be my people, and I will be their God.

EZEKIEL (593–571 B.C.) *Ezek. 37:21–23*

950. But Almighty God will, in His mercy, put an end to this chaos and a new age will begin. Then, said the Spirit, this is the beginning of the End of Time.

PROPHECY OF PREMOL (FIFTH CENTURY)

951. And I, John, saw the holy city, new Jerusalem, coming down from God out of heaven, prepared as a bride adorned for her husband. . . . And he carried me away in the spirit to a great and high mountain, and showed me that great city . . . descending out of heaven from God, having the glory of God: and her light was like unto a stone most precious, even like a jasper stone, clear as crystal; and had a wall great and high, and had twelve gates, and at the gates twelve angels, and names written thereon, which are the names of the twelve tribes of the children of Israel. . . . And the wall of the city had twelve foundations. . . And the city lieth foursquare and the length was as large as the breath. . . the wall thereof, an hundred and forty and four cubits, according to the measure of a man, that is, of the angel.

And the buildings of the wall of it was of jasper: and the city was pure gold, like unto clear glass. And the foundations of the wall of the city were garnished with all manner of precious stones, the first foundation was jasper; the second, sapphire; the third, a chalcedony; the fourth, an emerald; The fifth, sardonyx; the sixth, sardius; the seventh, chrysolyte; the eighth, beryl; the ninth, a topaz; the tenth, a chrysoprasus; the eleventh, a jacinth; the twelfth, an amethyst. And the twelve gates were twelve pearls; every several gate was of one pearl: and the street of the city was pure gold, as it were transparent glass.

And I saw no temple therein: for the Lord God Almighty and the Lamb [a code for Jesus at his second coming] are the temple of it. And the city had no need of sun, neither of the moon, to shine in it: for the glory of God did lighten it, and the Lamb is there light thereof. And the nations of them which are saved shall walk in the light of it: and the kings of the earth do bring their glory and honor into it. And the gates of it shall not be shut at all by day: for there shall be no night there.

And I, John, saw the holy city, new Jerusalem, coming down from God out of heaven, prepared as a bride adorned for her husband. And I heard a great voice out of heaven saying, Behold, the tabernacle of God is with men, and he will dwell with them, and they shall be his people, and God himself shall be with them, and be their God.

ST. JOHN OF PATMOS (a.d. 81–96)

Rev. 21:2, 10–25, 2–3

952. And God shall wipe away all tears from their eyes; and there shall be no more death, neither sorrow, nor crying, neither shall there be any more pain: for the former things are passed away.

ST. JOHN OF PATMOS (a.d. 81–96)

Rev. 21:4–5

953. [After the desolation of Scotland by a "horrid black rain"] the people [of the Scottish highlands] will then return and take undisturbed possession of the land of their ancestors.

BRAHAN SEER (1665)

Tula Reborn

Over eighteen hundred years before he set foot on North American soil, the Toltec mystic Kate-Zahl (Quetzalcoatl) was carried in his meditations into a visionary dream: he saw the skyline of Tula— the present-day Toltec ruins of Teotihuacan in Mexico—being transformed sometime in our distant future from a ruin into the richness of a religious city rebuilt by Homo novus:

954. The heavens parted and a rising golden sun shone down on another Tula. Plainly I could see the valley, but the city was one I knew not. I was lifted beyond the cold earth. No longer I saw the Age of Destruction. Gone was the terrible Age of Warfare. I was looking beyond the Age of Carnage. Walk with me through this Age of the Future.

Tula shines in all its glory, but the metals are types we know not. Loving hands have rebuilt the parkways, have paved the streets, have reconstructed the temples. There is a great building where the books are kept for the scholars, and many are those who come to read them.

Tula is a great center of culture. Shining again is my Father's temple. You will see again the same inscriptions which today your eyes are seeing, but now all people can read.

Come to the metropolis of the future. Here are buildings unlike those we fashion, yet they have breathless beauty. Here people dress in materials we know not, travel in manners beyond our knowledge, but more important than all this difference are the faces of the people. Gone is the shadow of fear and suffering, for man no longer sacrifices and he has outgrown the wars of his childhood. Now he walks full-statured toward his destiny—in the Golden Age of Learning.

QUETZALCOATL (a.d. 947)

THE DISTANT FUTURE

BEYOND THE TWENTY-FIRST CENTURY

955. I had been born again in 2100 A.D. in Nebraska. The sea apparently covered all of the western part of the country, as the city where I lived was on the coast. The family name was a strange one. At an early age as a child I declared myself to be Edgar Cayce who had lived two hundred years before. Scientists, men with long beards, little hair, and thick glasses, were called in to observe me. They decided to visit the places where I said I had been born, lived and worked, in Kentucky, Alabama, New York, Michigan, and Virginia. Taking me with them, the group of scientists visited these places in a long, cigar-shaped metal flying ship which moved at high speed. Water covered part of Alabama. Norfolk, Virginia, had become an immense seaport. New York had been destroyed either by war or an earthquake and was being rebuilt. Industries were scattered over the countryside. Most of the houses were of glass. Many records of my work as Edgar Cayce were discovered and collected. The group returned to Nebraska, taking the records with them to study. . . . These changes in the earth will come to pass, for the time and times and half times are at an end, and there begins those periods for the readjustments.

EDGAR CAYCE (D. 1945)

956. There will be peace, union and change.

Nostradamus (1557) *C9 Q66*

957. After their long trials and persecutions [by 2500 A.D.] the restored House of Israel and Judah, having learned so much from their own sufferings, will be in a position to appreciate the wrongs of other races, and will adjust these wrongs by the Balance of Divine Justice.

Cheiro (1931)
Cheiro's World Predictions

958. Within as little time as another two hundred years humanity will experience a diversifications of species it hasn't seen since prehistoric times. Colonization of different planets in our solar system alone will create Martian humans with more waif-like women and elfin males growing more delicate bone structures more in harmony with a gravitational pull two-thirds less strong than on Earth.

John Hogue (1995)

959. In a period of about five hundred years from now, the aftermath of the Great Armageddon will completely revolutionize our present ideas of nations, kingdoms or republics; a wonderfully organized Central Government in Palestine will radiate laws of life and humanity to the entire world.

960. The Soul of Design is, in itself, *perfection*. Therefore, even its most unconscious effort must be in the end to reproduce *itself in all things*. In obedience to this law, Man—the highest effort of Design on this sphere, is, by the upward urge of ages, *slowly ascending toward perfection*.

961. [By 2500 A.D.] Despised peoples [the Jews] will be given an equal chance with those who up to now have been the most favored. Just as in far gone ages when the sons of Joseph born in Egypt from an Egyptian wife were brought into the sacred circle of the Twelve Tribes, so the children of Ishmael and the sons of Ham will become recognized, and the Negro, the Arab, the Hindu, and the Yellow race, instead of being regarded as an enemy or a "peril," will be drawn into universal co-partnership whose purpose will be the uplifting of the entire human race *and the fulfillment of the Divine Design whose ultimate purpose is the perfection of all.*

> CHEIRO (1931)
> Cheiro's World Predictions

962. By the year 2531, the family will be completely replaced by test-tube conception.

> ALDOUS HUXLEY (1931)

963. Creatures which science took for granted as being extinct will be rediscovered alive.

> ATTRIBUTED TO JEANE DIXON (C. 1970S)

964. Ah, to have the body of youth with the wisdom of age. That is what we say today, but in the 2100s people will have to wrestle with the raging hormones of youth blinding their wisdom in the heat of horniness.

> JOHN HOGUE (1991)

965. Before the moon has finished her entire cycle [1889–2250], the Sun [twentieth century] and then Saturn [Aquarian Age] will come. According to the Celestial signs the reign of Saturn will come a second time [Capricorn Age], so that all is calculated, the world draws near to its final death-dealing cycle [the universal conflagration].

NOSTRADAMUS (1555)

Preface to Les Propheties

Saturn co-rules the Age of Aquarius (A.D. 2000–4000) and the one that follows, the Age of Capricorn (A.D. 4000–6000). The Capricorn epoch will see humankind either destroyed or transcending the material (earthly) plane. The thirty-seventh century after Christ will see this theme influencing the dying Aquarian Age. The key words for Capricorn are "utilize" or "restrict." The human race will need to use all its hard-earned lessons from the past or be destroyed by its near godlike power over mind and matter. The physical destruction of the earth by a cosmic source heralds the coming of the Capricorn Age. In his preface to his son, Nostradamus tells us that the world will end in 3797.

966. The world near the final period [A.D. 3797?], Saturn, again, will make a late return [Age of Capricorn, A.D. 4000–6000]: The empire is transferred toward the Brodde race.

NOSTRADAMUS (1555) *C3 Q92*

"Brodde" describes a dark skinned race. A distant future interpretation of this prophecy may imply they are either an alien race or the future Race of Tan. The latter is a description created by T. Lobsang Rampa in his prophecies for a day when all races of earth commingle and the colors of all the races together place the average human in a Polynesian-style body the color of creamy brown.

967. Before the universal conflagration the world will be deluged by many floods to such heights that there will remain scarcely any land not covered by water, and this will last for so long that everything will perish except the earth itself and the races which inhabit it. Furthermore, before and after these floods many nations shall see no rains and there will fall from the sky such a great amount of fire and meteors that nothing will remain unconsumed. All this will happen a short time before the final conflagration.

NOSTRADAMUS (1555)
Preface to Les Propheties

968. The world will be approaching a great conflagration, although, according to my calculations in my prophecies, the course of time runs much further.

NOSTRADAMUS (1557)
Epistle to Henry II

In his preface to his son, Nostradamus tells us that the human race will yet survive even this last conflagration—indicating that we will by then have colonized space.

969. For eleven more times the Moon will not want the Sun. Both raised and lessened in degree. And put so low that one will sew little gold: that after famine and plague the secret will be revealed.

NOSTRADAMUS (1555) *C4 Q30*

This mystical prophecy may date the number of grand astrological lunar cycles from the birth of Christ until the end of the world. If we multiply 354 years eleven times we get the year A.D. 3894. Time ends a little over a century after Nostradamus's predicted conflagration of the earth by the sun in 3797. However, if we begin the count from the end of lunar cycle that began in Nostradamus's day (1535–1889), human history continues at least past the year A.D. 5783, or near the end of the Age of Capricorn (A.D. 6000).

970. Weeds, cockroaches, and rats will be the species most likely to survive the next mass extinction. Who knows, the next great messiah of the next four-billion-year round of evolution may look like Mickey Mouse.

JOHN HOGUE (1991)

971. When twenty years of the Moon's reign have passed, another will take up its reign for seven thousand years. When the exhausted Sun takes up its cycle and gathers up its days, then my prophecy and threats will be accomplished.

NOSTRADAMUS (1555) *C1 Q48*

Fascination with the obscure prophecies of Nostradamus is approaching 450 years in running. The prophet himself predicts the length of his own legacy. Roussat believes the astrological lunar cycle mentioned above is that of 1535–1889. Twenty years after 1535 gives us *Les Propheties* publication date, 1555. This could extend his chronicle of human history to beyond the ninth millennium, far beyond the destruction of the earth and the colonization of other stars.

WHAT THE FUTURE BLESSES, TODAY'S CULTURE WILL FIND HARD TO SWALLOW

Nostradamus horrified his readers when he said that someday kings would no longer rule the realm and mobs of peasants would be in power. We call this democracy. If people were horrified four hundred years ago at what we today perceive as a blessing, what things horrify us today that people four centuries hence will find a blessing? Let's see:

Euthanasia Accepted

972. By the end of the twenty-first century, death by so-called natural causes will no longer exist. People will live as long as they wish. Short of accidental death, people will face the challenge of having to choose their time of death consciously. In less than twenty years the mainstream will consider Jack Kevorkian a pioneer and heroic figure, although his methods will still be criticized. The reason for this practice will be the excessive numbers of people on the planet.

The Death of Personal Culture in the Aquarian Age

973. The Age of Aquarius will not be an easy twenty-century run for ego and personality. By the end of its first seven hundred years, the global society will appear aloof and cool to us today. People living then will look upon our hallowed fights to preserve our egos, nourish our daily dramas and dissensions, and ride the continual seesaw of extremes—extreme love, hate, happiness, sadness, etc.—as a great waste of time and life force. It may take seven centuries before humanity understands that the real revolution comes from living in balance with nature and with one's inner nature.

The End of the Arts As We Know Them

974. With no drama in life, a blissful culture will make the distraction of dramas irrelevant. This doesn't mean that human beings of the distant future won't entertain and inspire themselves, but it will be in ways we cannot appreciate today.

The End of Religious Altruism

975. Religions will suffer a deflated sense of importance when much pain, hunger, war, disease—the stuff that makes the world an anti-life realm worthy of escape to a better world has faded away, put to an end by a new era balancing material science with the science of meditation.

The End of Natural Birth

976. Artificial wombs will exactly and biologically mimic those of mothers. Babies will not be some soulless freaks bred in test tubes, because people in the future will have made such breakthroughs in the new metaphysical sciences that the process of birth will no longer be an unconscious event for the one who will be born, nor will it be some kind of genetic Russian roulette for the parents. People of our times will be remembered as barbaric and selfish for conceiving children without prior knowledge of genetic defects and illnesses, just so we could say they were "ours" and from "our" bloodline. The people of the future will understand that the family of humanity is one.

The role of "parents" will undergo a complete transformation. Parents of the future will not need to be your congenital mother and father, even though they love and dedicate their lives to your growth. They love you enough to find the finest genetic material to fashion for you the healthiest body possible, even if that means that not one strand of DNA comes from either of them. Moreover, they can contact discarnate souls prior to conception of the body so that all three—the child and the parents—have agreed to be together in the creation of the new life. The child of the future will be in conscious contact with his or her parents before, during, and after he or she is in the womb for nine months.

The End of Eating

977. In the future human beings will draw their sustenance directly from light. This will bring on many dramatic and rapid changes in our body chemistry. For one thing, such direct light-energy nourishment does not require that we break down heavy matter through a digestive factory of 30 feet of intestines, a pancreas, kidneys, and what-not; nor will we need the organs for excrement. The Indian mystic Osho visualized a future human race that used medallions they clamped on their heads like hats for twenty minutes to receive one full twenty-four-hour day's requirement of nourishment and regeneration. This new technology would eventually lead to humans of the future to dispensing with their gastrointestinal organs the way doctors today routinely perform appendectomies. People will truly have wasplike waists in five hundred years. The end of digestive organs will also put an end to 80 percent of the body's diseases. We will supplement the loss of enjoying food with holographic and virtual-reality technology. In the distant future you can think gastronomic satisfaction and it is there.

The End of Race

978. In the coming five hundred years, human interbreeding of the races will lead to only one highly robust and tanned human world race. Once the distinction of color disappears, racism will go the way of the dinosaurs.

The End of Sex

979. Human beings will eventually evolve beyond having male or female genitalia and sexuality. But fear not, the rule of conscious evolution dictates that what is abandoned with awareness is replaced by something far more fulfilling. People will abandon being "men" and "women," because they finally discover that they are already both forces inside. They will discard the joys of sex, because they will uncover the secret of living twenty-four hours a day in a state of orgasm, uncaused and free of the necessity of the other to trigger it.

The End of Love

980. Love will end when hate ends. One cannot exist without the other. The people of tomorrow will discover a higher state than love—one we cannot even imagine today.

The End of Good and Evil

981. The people of the future will be more self-observant than we. They will see that many of the things we believe are opposites are in fact complementary. They will understand what we today cannot fathom: that evil and good are like intimate partners in a dysfunctional marriage. One needs the other to be a couple. In the distant future people will seek the transmoral state. They will strive to understand the opposites called good and evil from a deeper consciousness that acts as a third and transcendent state of being beyond good and evil.

The End of Places of Worship

982. In five hundred years the religions—as we adore and know and depend on them—will fade away. People of that distant day will be simply religious. Their connection to the divine is so intimate that it makes the need of temples, mosques, churches, and synagogues obsolete.

The End of Star Trekking

983. A thousand to two thousand years from now the last stubborn hold-outs of the galactic human civilization will end their travels through physical space. They will understand at last that the final frontier is not in the stars. The greatest and eternal destiny is consciousness. It is consciousness filling itself out of the void of itself. It may take an exhausting journey through a thousand worlds before space-faring humanity understands that wherever one goes in the universe it is always here and now, and we are the universe seeking itself, enlightening itself.

JOHN HOGUE, INTERPRETING A WIDE
VARIETY OF SEERS OF THE DISTANT
FUTURE (1999)

SPACE EXPLORATION AND THE FINAL FRONTIER

984. The attempt by NASA to send a probe to collect material from a comet in 2004 will cause a heated debate about whether we might be exposing our ecosystem to an unknown interstellar microbe that could cause a world plague.

985. The Galileo spacecraft will not orbit Jupiter "forever," as many scientists claim it will in 1999. A future space agency will retrieve it sometime after 2050 and place the relic in the Smithsonian Museum.

986. The focal point of political, economic, and social power in the nineteenth and twentieth centuries centered in the countries surrounding the Northern Atlantic rim. The twenty-first century will see the focus move to the Pacific rim. The twenty-second and twenty-third centuries will see civilization focus on the solar system's rim.

JOHN HOGUE (1999)

987. He will come to take himself [*to* or] *within* the corner of the Moon, where he will be taken and placed on alien land.

NOSTRADAMUS (1557) *C9 Q65*

Depending on the syntax of the French, either the prophecy foretells the moon landing when it says man is taken "to" the moon or it describes a future underground lunar base when it says man is taken "within" the moon.

988. There will be peace, union, and change. Estates and offices [that were] low [are] high, those high [made] very low. To prepare for a journey [into space?] torments the first [child]. War to cease [the millennium of peace?], civil processes, debates.

NOSTRADAMUS (1557) *C9 Q66*

989. Again will the holy temples be polluted, and plundered by the Senate of Toulouse, Saturn two, three cycles revolved, in April, May, people of the new heaven.

NOSTRADAMUS (1557) *C9 Q72*

This may be the closest Nostradamus comes to dating the first solid contact with an alien race: in the spring. He regularly mentions spring 2000 in his prophecies, perhaps implying that by the first spring of the new millennium we are about to resolve a half century of extraterrestrial visitations with indisputable proof that alien intelligent life exists.

990. Plague and disease will disappear by the twenty-second century, but nature will challenge us again with new illnesses when we enter galactic exploration. The diseases will come from other worlds.

991. UFO cranks of the 1950s declared they were space brothers from Venus. In five hundred years there will be Venusian human beings, the ancestors of earth colonists. They will live on a world terraformed into a vast semitropical, semidesert world.

992. Nostradamus in his distant future prophecies seems to predict two great interstellar migrations into space. The first migration heads toward the star systems of the constellation of Aquarius and is lost in some disastrous first contact with an alien life form with doglike appearance. The second exodus leads humanity to successfully colonize the star systems of the constellation of Cancer, wherein Nostradamus's history of the future implies a near infinite and prosperous history.

JOHN HOGUE (1994)

993. Because of the tormented seas [of space], the strange ship will [land] at an unknown port: Notwithstanding the signals from the branch of palm [a telecommunications dish], after death, pillage: good [birds] arriving late.

NOSTRADAMUS (1555) C1 Q30

994. The chief who will have conducted the infinite people, far from the skies of their own [world], consisting of customs and tongues alien.

NOSTRADAMUS (1555) *C1 Q98*

995. After human-caused near mass extinction will come rapid human evolution caused by space exploration, resuming around the end of the twenty-first century.

JOHN HOGUE (1994)

996. Too much the heavens weep for the androgynous procreation. Near the heavens [space] human blood shed: Because of death too late a great people re-created, late and soon comes the awaited help.

NOSTRADAMUS (1555) *C2 Q45*

This might imply a future war between cloned and naturally bred humans in space.

997. The sacred pomp will come to lower its wings, at the coming of the great legislator: He will raise the humble, he will vex the rebels.

None of his like will be born on this earth.

NOSTRADAMUS (1555) *C5 Q79*

Either a great world leader or a future human messiah will be born on another planet.

998. The feeble group will occupy the earth, those of the high place will make horrible cries. The large flock of the outer corner [of the galaxy?] will be troubled. It falls near D. nebro [the star system of Deneb] the intelligence papers discovered.

NOSTRADAMUS (1557) *C8 Q56*

In a distant future context this one may describe the decline and fall of a galactic human civilization.

999. The human realm of Angelic offspring, will cause its [his] realm to hold in peace and union: War captive halfway inside its [his] enclosure. For a long time peace will be maintained by them.

NOSTRADAMUS (1557) *C10 Q42*

Could it be here that a sixteenth-century man is trying to describe the time a space-faring humanity will genetically bond with a more highly evolved extraterrestrial humanoid race—"Angelic offspring"? Such a union will eventually bring a lasting peace on earth—and any new earths colonized by our distant descendants.

1000. Although the planet Mars will finish its orbits, at the end of the last age, it will start again. Some will assemble in Aquarius for several years, others [travel to the constellation] in Cancer for a longer and uninterrupted time and for ever more.

NOSTRADAMUS (1555)

Preface to Les Propheties

We close with Nostradamus giving us some indication that the human exodus to the constellation of Aquarius will not be as fruitful as the mission to the stars of Cancer, where it seems humans will build its permanent home. Perhaps they will be conscious of the eternity of the present, and therefore live beyond the interruptions of time itself. Thus, when you step out tonight for a breath of evening air, look heavenward to the stars that glitter in the constellation of Cancer, for somewhere around those distant and cool fires of coruscating diamond light there may dwell your distant, and enlightened, descendants.

COPYRIGHT ACKNOWLEDGMENTS